For Joanna

"I have great faith in a seed.
convince me that you have a seed there
and I am prepared to expect wonders"
- Henry David Thoreau

Vegetables

For the Irish Garden

Klaus Laitenberger

ISBN 978 0 9565063 0 6

Printed and bound in Ireland by Castle Print.
Illustrations by Dympna Driscoll
Victorian Images Courtesy of Thomas Etty Seeds Esq.
Photography Anna-Maya Pawlowski
Editing by Margaret Holland
Printed on recycled paper

This book is available from:
www.milkwoodfarm.com

or contact us on:
milkwood.farm@hotmail.com

Contents

Introduction

Vegetables A-Z

Introduction

When I came to Ireland in 1999, organic vegetable growing at home was just starting to become popular even though it was only a small number of people who took it up. This has completely changed in recent years. More and more people are now growing their own food again and the perception that organic gardening is only for hippies and aristocrats, is quite outdated.

As we all know, Ireland has a unique climate. It took me a few years to adjust the growing techniques I learned to this climate and soil. The main changes I made was to be patient, to delay sowing and planting and to grow on raised beds.

In the vegetable section of the book I give fairly accurate sowing dates despite the fact that each growing season and micro-climate is completely different. These dates have worked for me for many years in the North-West of Ireland. They always err on the late side.

If you live in a sunnier part of Ireland you can possibly adjust the sowings dates and get an earlier crop. From late May onwards

Ireland has extremely favourable growing conditions – long days, plenty of moisture and mild, but not too hot temperatures. There is rarely a need to waste your time with a watering can.

'Organic' must be one of the words most bandied about in recent years. People are confused as to what it actually means. They are mystified as to its exclusivity until they turn that first sod in their little vegetable plot and realise it's the most natural thing in the world to sow, gather and eat the best of nature's gifts from outside your back door.

Now with the endless talk of our allergies and sicknesses people are thinking twice about food, how it is produced, and where it comes from, often travelling thousands of miles to our local shops.

In the end home grown organic food has to be better. The very idea that we see what we have planted where it is growing and knowing that we pick it fresh daily and bring it to our table to be eaten within half an hour. The digging, weeding and composting is surely worth it; not to mention the time driving, parking and queuing for the alternative.

Growing your own food can save you a substantial amount of money. From a 200sqm plot you can save up to €1,000 in vegetable purchases. The garden can be an extension to your house: it's a larder providing you with food, a wood store, a place to dry your clothes on the line, a playground for your children, a restful green patch to sit and chat, a place to read and entertain in – all outside your door. And don't forget it's also the place where millions of other creatures live quietly getting on with their life's purpose.

It is hard to believe how we have become estranged from the land around us. Yet not that long ago (in terms of human evolution) we were completely dependant on what the earth could bear. This dependence brought about a very close connection between us humans and the earth around us. As hunters and gatherers (99% of our time on earth) everything was provided for us – we lived in a garden of Eden. Then life got a bit harder when we started to cultivate crops and tended to animals. We had to work a lot harder. We had to plough the soil, cultivate the crops and grind the seeds. Was this the time when we were thrown out of paradise?

Farming started around 10,000 years ago (less than 1% of our time on earth) in the Fertile Crescent in countries such as Iraq, Afghanistan, Southern Turkey and Jordan.

The move away from agriculture only began with the onset of the industrial revolution and chemical farming only prospered after the second world war when there was a sudden surplus of chemicals which were used for bombs and what better use was there than to spread them on the land?

And now there is only a small minority of people involved in agriculture (less than 3% in Ireland) who have the responsibility to produce food us. The rest of the population has lost this vital thread to our past. I think it is absolutely crucial to reconnect with this important link even on the smallest scale just to be able to appreciate the constant miracles of observing a seed germinate or to dig a few potatoes.

In the last few decades we perceive ourselves as a separate unit on the earth and think that technology will eventually solve all our problems. But I strongly believe that only the care for the earth and the soil and especially the plots we tend will bring us a lot more satisfaction and happiness than the many unnecessary gadgets which seem all important to us now.

Artichoke, Globe

Latin name:
Cynara scolymus
Family:
Compositae (also known as
Asteraceae)
Related to:
Lettuce, chicory, endive,
Jerusalem artichoke.
Botanical classification:
Cynara derives from the Greek
kyon, a dog, with reference to the
spines suggesting dog's teeth.

Introduction
Globe artichokes are one of the
most prized garden vegetables.
They are perennials and are well
suited in your flower border where
they make beautiful specimens.

Globe artichokes will grow to
about 1.8m tall with a spread of
1.2m in diameter, another reason
why they are not suitable for a
small vegetablegarden. Their
lifespan is about 5 years.

History
It is one of the world's oldest
cultivated vegetables, grown by the
Greeks and the Romans. It was
introduced to northern Europe in
the early sixteenth century both as
a vegetable and an ornamental
plant in monastery gardens.

Soil and site
Globe artichokes prefer a fertile,
well-drained soil with plenty of sun
and some shelter from strong
winds.

Sowing and planting
If you already have an established
plant, it is very easy to propagate
them from suckers which appear at
the base of the mother plant. In
early spring, dig gently around the
base to expose the suckers and cut
them off with a sharp knife. Plant
them out into their final position

about 1m apart.

If you do not have an established plant you can also raise the plants from seed. Sow the seeds in March individually into small pots (5cm) and place them on the windowsill or a small propagator (at 18°C). Keep them in a warm place until May. If they outgrow their pots you will need to pot them on into bigger pots (10cm). After hardening off you can plant them into their final position 1m apart. Sometimes they produce heads in their first year.

Spacing
Between plants: 1 metre
Between rows: 1 metre

Rotation
The globe artichoke is a perennial vegetable so it should not be included in your vegetable rotation.

Plant care
Every year in spring you should spread well decomposed compost around the base of the plants.
I found that cutting back the flowering stalks at the base, as soon as possible after harvesting the heads, will promote the growth of strong suckers which will produce a heavy yield in the following year.

Harvesting and storing
The plants should produce ripe flower heads from June until early August. The heads should be harvested when they are still closed otherwise they become tough.

Potential problems
Luckily globe artichokes are not affected by pests or diseases.

How much to grow?
Each plant may yield up to six heads and it takes up 1 m² so it really is only a delicacy, certainly not a productive crop.

Varieties
Green Globe (large green heads)
Purple Globe (purple heads, very hardy)
Imperial Star (an improved Green Globe variety, produces artichokes in the first season)
Violetta di Chioggia (purple heads, very ornamental)

Cardoon

Cardoon (*Cynara cardunculus* var. *edulis*) is a very close relative of the globe artichoke. The two are in fact very difficult to distinguish. The cardoon, however, is grown for its blanched leaf stalks. It used to be a common vegetable in Victorian times and it is now making a slow comeback. I must confess, though, I have often grown it for its ornamental value but I never blanched the stalks and eaten it.

"His memoir is a splendid artichoke of anecdotes, in which not merely the heart and leaves but the thistles as well are edible"
- John Leonard

Artichoke, Jerusalem

Latin name:
Helianthus tuberosus
Family:
Compositae (also known as
Asteraceae)
Related to:
Lettuce, endive, chicory, globe
artichoke.
Botanical classification:
Helianthus derives from the Greek
helios, the sun, and *anthos,* a flower.

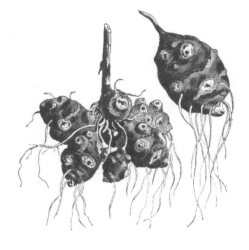

Introduction

The Jerusalem artichoke is
definitely one of the easiest
vegetables to grow. It is grown
for its edible tubers which have the
appearance of a knobbly potato.
The variety 'Fuseau' is the least
knobbly type. Unlike the potato it
is completely free of any diseases.
The Jerusalem artichoke is
extremely high yielding and can
grow in relatively poor soil.
It is very similar to the sunflower.
In hot summers you may even get
small sunflowers on the plant. The
name 'Jerusalem' has nothing to do
with the place. It was simply a
false interpretation from the Italian
Girasola articiocco, the sunflower
artichoke. *Girasola* means 'turning
to the sun'. For some reason this
corruption of the word has stayed
until today.
I am always surprised why more
people do not grow this vegetable.
I know the flavour is not always
agreeable to everyone but it is very
nutritious. It can have an antisocial
effect, hence often nicknamed
'fartichoke'!

History

It is a native of the North
American plains and has been
cultivated by the Indians. It has
been grown in Europe since 1640.

Soil and site

Jerusalem artichokes can thrive in
almost any soil but obviously, the
more fertile the soil, the higher the
yield.
Some gardeners use Jerusalem
artichokes as a windbreak. In very

exposed sites you could put fence posts at either end of the row and a plain wire across it. This will prevent them from falling.

Planting

When planting the tubers it is important to select the best ones. If you continually select the least knobbly seed tubers your strain may improve. It is important that you plant them as early in the year as possible, as soon as you can get the bed ready (February-March). They are very hardy plants.

Spacing

I grow them exactly like potatoes in drills. If you have more than one drill, space the drills 90cm apart (from centre to centre). I plant them 30cm apart in the drill and about 15cm deep. There is always the question which way round should you plant. Ideally plant with the growth point up but it really does not matter, as they will grow anyway.

Rotation

Jerusalem artichokes have no specific pest or disease problem, so you do not need to be strict about crop rotation. They can be safely grown on the same plot of land.

Plant care

During the growing season I earth up the plants twice by dragging or shovelling soil from the path onto the stems. This makes them steadier and also increases the yield.

Harvesting and storing

You can start digging out tubers from late autumn right through the winter. Alternatively you can dig out the whole crop and store the tubers in boxes of moist sand (see p230). This way they will last until the following April.

Any tuber left behind will create a weed problem the following year. You should fork over the bed twice after harvesting the tubers as you will find more hiding away. It is probably better not to include Jerusalem artichokes in the rotation and grow them at the end of your vegetable plot where they can act as a windbreak. Due to their healthy growth there is no need to rotate them. It is not advisable though to leave them permanently in the ground and let all the tubers re-sprout. You will just end up with thousands of tiny tubers.

Potential problems

The only problem you could possibly have is hares eating the young stalks in early spring. This can easily be prevented by using netting or a cloche which can be removed when the plants are established by the end of April.

How much to grow?

For a newcomer to Jerusalem artichokes, 5 plants are more than sufficient as each tuber will yield around 2-3kg of artichokes.

Varieties

Fuseau (long, smooth, white tubers, excellent yield)
Gerard (round, red, slightly knobbly tubers, very good yield)
Dwarf Sunray (short stemmed variety which is highly ornamental, flowers freely)

"The highest reward for a person's toil is not what they get for it, but what they become by it"
— John Ruskin

Asparagus

Latin name:
Asparagus officinalis
Family:
Asparagaceae
Botanical classification:
Derived from the ancient Greek; *a*, intensive, and *sparasso*, to tear, alluding to the prickles of some spcies. *Officinalis*, of shops.

Introduction
Asparagus is such a delicacy and such an attractive plant that it is well worth growing at home. However, it has a cropping season of only six weeks and, being a perennial, it takes up valuable space for the rest of the year. It also takes three years after planting before you get a reasonable yield but then it will produce shoots (spears) for the next 20 years.
I would choose a modern variety which is an all-male F1 hybrid.

They are a lot more vigorous than the older varieties.

History
Asparagus has been grown for over 2000 years. The Romans believed that the spears arose from rams' horns buried in the ground. The wild forms of asparagus grow in Europe, Asia and North Africa.

Soil and site
Asparagus prefers a fertile, well-drained soil with plenty of sun and some shelter from strong winds. The ideal pH is between 6.3 and 7.5. If your soil is heavy it is best to grow them in traditional raised beds with plenty of compost added to them.

Sowing and planting
You can either raise asparagus from seed or buy young plants which are called crowns. I always prefer to buy good quality crowns as they reach maturity a year earlier than seed grown asparagus.
Plant the crowns in early spring in

single or double rows (depending on the size of the raised bed).

Dig a trench 30cm wide and 20cm deep. Then dig in well-rotted manure or compost and cover with 5cm of good topsoil. Make a 10cm high ridge in the centre of the trench and place the crowns on the ridge 30cm apart. The roots have to be spread out evenly. Then you fill in with good soil so that the crown tips are just visible. You can then mulch the crown surface with a shallow layer of well-rotted compost (ideally a weed free compost). If you have a double row allow 60cm between the rows.

Spacing

Between plants: 30cm
Between rows: 60cm

Rotation

Asparagus is a perennial vegetable so it cannot be included in your vegetable rotation.

Plant care

Keep asparagus beds weed free at all times. Once you get perennial weeds such as scutch grass or bindweed into the beds they are impossible to get rid of as you can't fork the roots of the weeds out once the plants are established.

Every year in early spring spread a mulch of well-decomposed weed free compost or manure (about 5cm deep) over the beds. It is probably safer to buy composted manure or compost which is weed free. I always use Envirogrind compost for this purpose.

The tall ferny shoots will have to be supported with canes and ties, otherwise they will fall over. They are very important as they produce the food for the following year's crop.

In October when the foliage has turned yellow cut them off about 3cm above the soil.

Harvesting and storing

You should not harvest asparagus in the first two years after planting, to help get the plants established and strong for the future years.

In the third year you can start to harvest the spears (young shoots) from May onwards, but only one or two from each plant. From the fourth year onwards they will be fully productive and produce about 12 spears per plant. You carefully cut the spears with a sharp knife about 2cm below ground level when they are about 15cm high. During the 6-week harvesting period you should check the plants every three to four days otherwise they will quickly grow too big and become tough. Every spring you can add a 5cm layer of good top-soil, sand and compost mix before the spears appear.

Potential problems

Asparagus is not affected by any specific pests or diseases. The main general pests are slugs and snails who adore the young shoots of asparagus. It is important to control these molluscs especially in spring.

How much to grow?

Ten plants are sufficient for a generous weekly helping for the six-week harvesting period from year four onwards.

Varieties

Connover's Colossal (old variety, suitable for light soils, good yield)
Jersey Knight F1 (high yield, an all-male variety, suitable for heavy soils)
Martha Washington (American variety, good yield)

"Asparagus inspires gentle thoughts"
- Charles Lamb

Bean, Broad

Latin name:
Vicia faba
Family:
Leguminosae
Related to:
Peas, French and runner beans, clover, vetch.
Botanical classification:
Vicia is a classical Latin name derived from *vincio*, to bind.

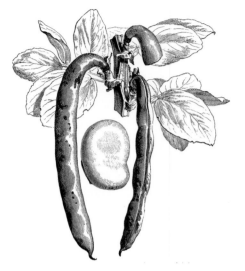

Introduction
Broad beans are an excellent beginner's vegetable. They are very easy to grow and are also very hardy (up to −8° C) and reliable. They have an upright growth habit.

History
Broad beans are one of the earliest plants to be cultivated by mankind. They have been an important crop since the Stone Age. Broad beans were well known in the ancient cultures of Egypt, Greece, Italy and many Middle Eastern countries. The ancient Greeks dedicated the broad beans to Apollo and believed that over-indulgence dulled the senses. Dioscorides wrote that they are the causes of troublesome dreams.

Soil and site
Broad beans do best on an open site, as aphid infestation is thus minimised. Aphids spread rapidly in sheltered places.
The soil should be well dug and reasonably fertile - manured from the previous crop. Too much nitrogen will inhibit nitrogen fixation from the air through rhizobium bacteria. The soil pH should be between 5.5 and 7.

Sowing
Autumn types:
Sow directly 5cm deep in drills outdoors from late September until early November.
Spring types:
Sow directly 5cm deep in drills outdoors from late February until late April.

Spacing
Between plants: 15cm
Between rows: 45cm

Rotation
Broad beans should be rotated around the garden so that follow on crops will benefit from the nitrogen they fixed.

Plant care
Support:
Smaller varieties generally do not need support. Taller ones, however, may need a support of canes and string that prevent them from falling over. (See diagram)

Harvesting
Overwintered crops may be ready for harvesting from May onwards. Early spring sowings will be cropping from June until August. Harvest the pods as soon as the seeds are fully formed but before they become mealy. Young small pods (2.5cm) can be picked and eaten young.
After cropping has finished, cut and remove the tops leaving the roots in the ground to allow the nitrogen fixing nodules to rot down and release their nitrogen.

Storing
Broad bean seeds can be blanched and deep- frozen or dried.

Example of a good support:

Potential problems
Black bean aphid (commonly known as blackfly) is the most common pest, attacking mainly the new soft growth at the top of the plant, especially in summer. When plants are fully grown, the tops can be nipped out.
The pea and bean weevils will notch the leaves of broad beans but this has very little effect on the yield, so no treatment is necessary. The black bean seed fly lays its eggs in freshly prepared soil and the maggots will feed on the seeds and seedlings. Mice may eat seeds and seedlings. Pre-germination of seeds lessens the problem as establishment is faster. Chocolate spot is characterised by small brown spots on the leaves, stems and pods. The over-wintered crops will have produced many beans before the disease sets in during summer. As a preventative ensure there is adequate drainage and good soil fertility.

How much to grow?

Broad beans take up a lot of space, so they may not be the most suitable crops for small gardens.

A two-metre bed of broad beans will approximately yield 6kg of beans.

Varieties

Autumn types:
Aquadulce Claudia (the most reliable variety for autumn sowing)
Super Aquadulce (early, hardy, recommended for autumn sowing)
Spring types:
Bunyard's Exhibition (long pods, good yield and flavour, very reliable)
Express (very early, high yield, very tasty)
Witkeim (excellent variety, large number of medium seized pods)
Speciality types:
Grando Violetto (unusual heritage variety with purple beans)
Red Epicure (very old variety, crimson flower, highly decorative)
The Sutton (an extra dwarf variety for windswept gardens)

"I came to love my rows, my beans, though so many more than I wanted. They attached me to the earth, and I got strength like Antaeus"
- Henry David Thoreau

Bean, French

Latin name:
Phaseolus vulgaris
Family:
Leguminosae
Related to:
Runner beans, broad beans, peas, clovers.
Botanical classification:
Phaseolus is an ancient name. It includes a wide range of annuals and perennials. *Vulgaris* means common.

Introduction

French beans are tender annuals. There are climbing and bushy types. The whole pods can be eaten when immature. There is great variation in pod types: green, yellow, purple or speckled. They may be flat, round, pencil shaped, long or short. The dwarf French beans grow to about 40cm high with 25-30cm spread.
Climbing types may grow over 2.4m high.

History

French beans originate from Central and South America. They grow wild in mountains at 500-2000m. They were domesticated in ancient times, but have only been introduced to Europe and Asia at the time of the Spanish conquest. They were introduced to northern parts of Europe in the early 16th century.

Soil and site

French beans require a very sunny and sheltered site. The soil should be fertile, moisture-retentive and free-draining. The soil pH can be slightly acidic ranging from 5.5-7.
If you do not have a sheltered garden it is wise not to grow the climbing French beans. Runner beans and dwarf French beans would be more suitable.

Sowing
Climbing French beans

Seeds can either be sown indoors for planting out later, or sown directly into the ground.
Indoor sowing:
Sow 5 seeds into 9cm pots in the third week of May. The sowing

21

depth is 4cm. The plants should then be hardened off a month later (for about a week) and can then be planted around a climbing frame (bamboo canes or hazel).

Outdoor Sowing:
You can also sow 5 seeds around each cane of your climbing frame. The safest time for this is from mid May until June. The seeds need a
minimum soil temperature of 12°C.

Dwarf French beans
Once the soil temperature is warm enough the seeds will germinate very reliably. If you can wait until late May there is no need to raise the plants in pots indoors. They can be sown directly 4cm deep in drills.

Spacing
Dwarf French beans
Between plants: 15cm
Between rows: 40cm

Climbing French beans
Canes are placed 30cm apart along the row with the rows 60cm apart. Sow 5 seeds around each cane.

Rotation
Whilst not necessary to rotate beans, it is most beneficial for any follow-on crop because legumes have the ability to fix atmospheric nitrogen.

Plant care
Climbing varieties need a climbing support: either a wigwam (see diagram below) or traditional frames using bamboo canes or hazel rods. Keep the bed weed free and help the odd straggler up the cane. Most of the shoots usually find their way up themselves.

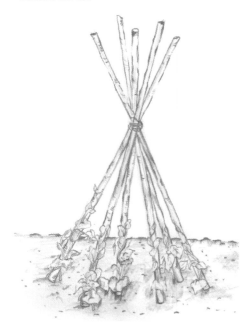

Harvesting
French beans can be harvested from July until the first frost. The pods should be picked regularly (once or twice a week), so they are still tender. If you do not harvest regularly the plant puts all its energy into ripening the seeds at the expense of new flowers and beans.

So even if you are completely fed up with them they should still be picked if you want your crop to continue. If the pods are too old, they tend to be stringy. Modern varieties, however, are bred to be stringless.

Storing
French beans are best eaten fresh. If you have a glut of them, you can blanch and freeze them for the winter months (see p231).

Potential problems
Slugs can be a big problem, especially when plants are young. Other pests include root aphids, black bean aphid and bean seed fly. Diseases include foot and root rots, halo blight and viruses.
With good cultural practices (rotation, good healthy fertile soil, healthy seeds, resistant varieties) these problems can be overcome.

How much to grow?

Climbing French beans
Because it's a risky crop I would only grow one wigwam with 5 or 6 canes tied together at the top. If they grow healthy you may get about 5-7 kg of beans throughout the season.

Dwarf French beans
A 5m long bed with a triple row of beans will yield about 7kg.

Varieties
Dwarf types:
Cropper Tepee (green pods, excellent taste, pods are above the leaves)
Lazy Housewife (an old heritage variety)
Purple Teepee (purple pods, excellent taste, pods are above the leaves)
Royalty (dark purple pods, excellent taste, high yield)
Safari (vigorous, disease resistant, pods are above the leaves)

Climbing types:
Hunter (flat podded, stringless, very high yield over long period)
Blue Lake (pencil podded, very high yield)
Eva (oval shaped pods)
Barlotto Lingua di Fuoco ('Firetongue', highly decorative with green pods speckled with red splashes)
Cobra (dark green, tender bean. The pods are long, round and stringless)

"This is the germinal spot of gathering green.
A close-curled, blissful fist
Of dreaming bean, milk-wet opal in the pod"
- Katherine Pierpoint

23

Bean, Runner

Latin name:
Phaseolus coccineus
Family:
Leguminosae
Related to:
French beans, broad beans, peas, clover.
Botanical classification:
Phaseolus is the ancient Greek name for beans. *Coccineus* means scarlet. It includes a wide range of annuals and perennials.

Introduction
Runner beans are much more prolific and reliable than climbing French beans and do much better outdoors in Ireland. They are also very decorative. The pods are long and flat. They are mostly climbing types, but a few dwarf (bush) varieties also exist. To me this seems a contradiction in terms – 'dwarf runner beans'.
Despite their relatively easy cultivation they are not very popular in Ireland.

History
Runner beans are native to Central America. They were originally introduced into Europe as an ornamental flowering plant in the middle of the 17th century.

Soil and site
Runner beans prefer a deep, rich, fertile soil with plenty of compost or composted manure dug in. A sheltered but sunny site is ideal. Be careful what you plant next to the beans as they will cause a lot of shade on the north side for the

other plants.
Research has shown that adding well-rotted farmyard manure when preparing the soil can increase the yield by 57%.

Sowing

Seeds can either be sown indoors for planting out later or sown directly into the ground.
Only one sowing is necessary as the crop produces over a long time especially if it is well managed.

Indoor sowing:

Sow 5 seeds into 9cm pots in the third week of May. The sowing depth is 5cm. The plants should then be hardened off a month later (for about a week) and you can then plant one pot containing the five plants next to each cane of the climbing frame.

Outdoor sowing:

Alternatively, you can sow 5 seeds around each cane of your climbing frame. The safest time for this is mid May until June. The seeds need a minimum soil temperature of 10°C to germinate.

Spacing

A double row 70cm apart with canes 40cm apart in the row and 5 plants per cane will give you good yields of runner beans.

Rotation

Rotation is the same as with other beans.

Plant care

Watering:

Research has shown that watering the soil during dry spells will greatly increase the yield. Research also found that the old fashioned practice of misting the flowers with water actually decreases the development of the pods.

Training:

Most runner beans are climbers and really need sturdy climbing supports. There is nothing worse than waking up at night wondering if your beans are still standing especially if they are just starting to produce.
See diagram on following page.

In the first few weeks you may need to help the shoots to grow along the canes, but after that they will be fine. If they have not found their way up, the shoots can be tied loosely to the canes. When they reach the top of the climbing support, the growing tip should be nipped out. I must admit I rarely do this unless I'm worried that they will get too top heavy and collapse.

Pod stripping:

Experiments showed that if the plant is stripped of all pods in early August later yield will be quadrupled. So you should remove all the pods before you go on holidays.

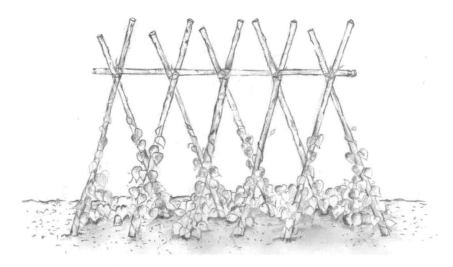

Example of a climbing frame

Harvesting

The beans are ready from July onwards until about mid October. Once they crop they should be thoroughly picked at least once or twice a week. You should harvest the beans while they are still tender before the seeds begin to swell in the pods. The more they are picked, the more they will produce. Therefore, it is important to remove all the beans that have been overlooked during the previous harvest.

If the beans are left longer on the plants the majority of them would become tough and possibly stringy and the plants may stop flowering.

Thus the yield will be dramatically reduced. So it is well worth letting your friends clear the crop when you are on holidays. Modern varieties are bred to be less stringy or completely stringless. I would recommend growing these varieties as it could be off-putting biting into a stringy runner bean.

Storing

French beans are best eaten fresh. If you have a glut, you can blanch and freeze them for the winter months (see p231).

Potential problems

Slugs are the only serious pests which attacks runner beans, especially when the plants are still small. Grey mould (botrytis) can become a problem in damp and cool conditions.

Crooked beans are a common problem. These often result where the young bean touches the leaves or the supports. This problem occurs more frequently on exposed sites.

Short beans are often produced in hot weather as it hastens the beans' ripening, thus stopping the lengthening of pod.

How much to grow?
One wigwam, which roughly occupies 1 m², can produce up to 10kg of runner beans.

Varieties
Enorma (very large pods, very high yield, with good flavour)
Lady Di (prolific cropper with an excellent nutty flavour)
Scarlet Emperor (excellent flavour and texture, attractive red flowers)

Runner beans with highly decorative qualities:
Roquencourt (stunning blue beans)
Painted Lady (red and white flowers, excellent flavour when harvested young)

Dwarf variety:
Hammond's Dwarf (only suited for container gardening)

Tip
Some Native American tribes let the beans climb up maize plants, but sunflowers could also be used.
It is important to let the support plants grow to about a metre before planting the beans at the base.

"Nine bean rows will I have there, a hive for the honey-bee,
And live alone in the bee-loud glade".
- W.B. Yeats

Beetroot

Latin name:
Beta vulgaris
Family:
Chenopodiaceae (Goosefoot Family)
Related to:
Chard, perpetual spinach, sugar beet and annual spinach.
Botanical classification:
Beta is the Latin term for beetroot; or from the Celtic *bett*, meaning red. *Vulgaris* means common.

Introduction
Beetroot are delicious and very easily grown vegetables. From just two sowings you can get an eight months' supply of roots. They do not suffer from any pests or diseases. The secret is to avoid any growth check otherwise the plants may bolt or become woody. If you haven't eaten home-grown beetroot yet you will be in for a treat.

History
Beetroot originates from Northern Africa and Western Asia and was used as a food plant for at least 2000 years.
The Romans introduced the beetroot into Northern Europe. The Celts grew a white beetroot (*Beta rapa*). Red Beetroot was first mentioned in the 13th century in northern Italy. It was only in the 17th century that the red beetroot became the main type in Europe.

The wild beet, *Beta vulgaris* subsp. *maritima* is a common seaside plant in south and west Europe.

Types
The most popular beetroot is the red and round (known as globe) type, but there are also yellow and white types available. There are also long cylindrical beetroot. These are ideal for pickling as all the slices are the same size. They also tend to be higher yielding.

Soil and site

Beetroot prefers light, well-drained soil. Fresh manure application before sowing should be avoided. A dressing of old compost incorporated in early spring is very beneficial.

Beetroot is one of the easiest vegetables to grow so even on heavy soil you can grow excellent beetroot, provided you have raised beds to improve drainage.

Sowing

It is very important to remember that most beetroot seeds are clusters of more than one seed. This means if you sow one seed, you will have three to five seedlings germinating. These have to be thinned to one seedling soon after germination otherwise the beetroots will remain very small. Some modern varieties are available as monogerm seeds. This means that they only contain a single seed so saving work on thinning.

Early varieties for summer use can be sown directly outside in a well prepared seed bed in shallow drills (1.5cm). I never had much success with the early sowings in March. The earliest I would start is in late April but you get a much better crop in May. For the early sowing in April make sure you use a bolt-resistant variety such as 'Boltardy'.

Some gardeners prefer to raise the seedlings in large modular trays. If you try this method make sure that you plant the seedlings out when they are still quite small. I always found beetroot very easy to sow directly outside as the seeds are large enough, easy to handle and I do not want to clutter up valuable propagation space.

Maincrop varieties are best sown directly outside like the early crop in the last two weeks in May or even into June. During that time they germinate very quickly (7-10 days) and grow very fast. The reason for getting woody, tough beetroot is often slow growth.

Spacing

Early crop:
Final spacing-
Between plants: 10cm
Between rows: 20cm

Main crop:
Final spacing-
Between plants: 10cm
Between rows: 25cm

I initially sow the seeds about 2.5cm apart and then thin them in two stages. The first thinning is done a couple of weeks after germination. I remove all unwanted seedlings from the clusters (not for monogerm varieties) and leave one seedling every 5cm.
The thinnings rarely do well when

transplanted. If you have gaps in the rows you are better off sowing a few new seeds.

When they reach the baby beetroot stage you can harvest every second plant. These are delicious and you can also cook the leaves like spinach.

This allows the remaining plants to fully develop. If you want to grow large beetroot you can increase the spacing to 15cm between plants

Rotation

Beetroot and other members of the goosefoot family are not prone to any specific pests or diseases so you do not have to be too fussy about rotation. You could use them as 'flexi-crops' or gap fillers.

Plant care

Apart from keeping the crop weed free and properly thinned to the required spacing, there is no other maintenance required.

Harvesting

Early beetroot can be harvested throughout the summer at whatever size you prefer them or whenever you want some beetroot. It is best to twist off the leaves to avoid damage and bleeding of the roots.

Maincrop beetroot for storage should be left until October. Of course, if you want to eat some before then, there is no problem, but if you grow some for storing, you should let them mature until

October.

Storing

Beetroot is an excellent winter vegetable and stores extremely well in boxes of damp sand (see page 230). One year I had beetroot until May of the following year and they were still as good as freshly harvested roots.

Potential problems

Beetroot is one of the easiest vegetables to grow. There is no specific pest or disease that affects it. Slugs may eat young seedlings especially if sown too early or if the garden is a bit wild but generally they would go for the other vegetables first.

Beetroot is very sensitive to a deficiency of boron in the soil. The symptoms are brown sunken patches on the roots and black areas inside the root.

How much to grow?

If you eat 3 reasonable sized beetroot per week, storing from October until the end of April (28 weeks) you will need 84 beetroot. So if you space them 10cm apart in the row and you fit 4 rows in a bed (bed width: 1.2m) you will get 40 beetroot per metre.

In only 2 metres of your bed you can grow enough beetroot to give you a few roots for 28 weeks!

Varieties

My favourite variety of beetroot is 'Pablo F1'. I have grown them for the last few years and I have given up experimenting with other varieties because this one is just perfect. In case you cannot get 'Pablo' you can try:

Detroit Globe (dark red flesh)
Boltardy (bolt resistant, early variety)
Cylindra (cylindrical shape)
Egyptian Turnip Rooted (heritage variety)

If you want something unusual try:
Barbietola di Chioggia (an Italian variety with unusual white and red alternating internal rings)
There are also white (Albina Vereduna) and golden (Burpee's Golden) varieties available.

"Let food be your medicine and medicine be your food"
- Hippocrates

Broccoli, sprouting

Latin name:
Brassica oleracea Italica Group
Family:
Brassicaceae (also known as
Cruciferae)
Related to:
Brussels sprouts, kale, cauliflower,
cabbage, swede, turnip, radish,
cress.
Botanical classification:
Brassica derives from the Celtic
bresic, the name for cabbage.
Oleracea means 'as a herb' – the
wild cabbage.

Introduction

Sprouting broccoli is an extremely
useful vegetable as it matures in
late winter to early spring during
the hungry gap period when there
is very little else around.
The name broccoli derives from
the Latin *brachium* which means
'branch'. In the 17th century it
was referred to as 'Sprout
Cauliflower' and 'Italian
Asparagus'.
There is still confusion about its
name. What consumers call
broccoli is really called calabrese.
So if you want the green, dense
curd which has become very
fashionable in recent years. But if
you want to grow this delicious
vegetable with mostly purple and

sometimes white flowering shoots,
read on.

History

Broccoli most likely originated in
Greece. The first records of
broccoli date from the first century
AD.
It then spread from Italy to
northern Europe but only arrived
in England in the 18th century.

Soil and site

Sprouting broccoli requires a
fertile, deep soil with high
moisture retention and good
drainage.
Sprouting broccoli is easy to grow
and will tolerate most sites, even

fairly exposed ones as long as adequate support is provided. Poorer soils can be improved by a fairly heavy application of half rotted manure or compost, ideally in the previous autumn, so that the soil can settle down. The pH level of the soil should be above 6.5 otherwise it should be corrected either in the form of calcified seaweed or ground limestone. An acid soil may encourage the spread of clubroot.

Sowing

Many beginners sow sprouting broccoli far too early and then the plants get confused and may produce in autumn or become too big to survive the winter. The best time to sow is in mid June.

You can sow sprouting broccoli in modular trays which are placed in a greenhouse (or tunnel). I sow one or two seeds per module about 1.5cm deep. If two seeds germinate you have to remove the weaker seedling. They usually germinate within 5 to 7 days and are ready for planting out about 4 weeks after sowing.

In order to prolong the harvesting season you can sow an early and a late variety at the same time.

Spacing

Sprouting broccoli becomes quite a large plant so do not underestimate the space it requires. A spacing of 75cm each way is the minimum.

Rotation

It is absolutely essential to keep sprouting broccoli in the brassica section of your rotation to prevent a build up of the numerous brassica pests and diseases.

Plant care

Sprouting broccoli gets very top heavy so they will benefit from a generous earthing up. In exposed gardens you may need to stake the plants to prevent them collapsing during the winter gales. But be warned: bamboo canes do not work for this purpose. You would need to drive in a 4 x 4cm thick square peg or an old strong tool handle.

Harvesting and storing

Harvest sprouting broccoli when the heads appear but well before they open up into yellow flowers. The plants mature around February and sometimes produce into May.

The shoots should be cut when they are about 15cm long. It is absolutely crucial that they are harvested regularly and that they are not allowed to go into flower. If this happens still cut them off and discard and they will produce new shoots.

Broccoli can be stored in a plastic bag in the fridge for 3 to 4 days or it can be blanched and frozen.

Potential problems

Sprouting broccoli is susceptible to the same pests and diseases as cabbage and the same control measures are recommended.

How much to grow?

Given the fact that they require a lot of space and a long growing period, (9 months) I suggest you grow 3-4 plants. They will produce enough for a family during the harvesting season.

Varieties

There are now excellent varieties of sprouting broccoli around.

Purple varieties:

Purple Sprouting Early or Late
Red Arrow (late, improved variety)
Red Spear (improved variety)

White varieties:

White Star

Other types of broccoli
Bordeaux F1

This is an annual broccoli which produces heads after only 4 to 5 months after sowing. I have grown it for a number of years and I think it has an exceptional flavour.

It is actually a cross between purple sprouting broccoli and calabrese.

You can sow it from April until June in modular trays (1 seed per cell) and plant out 4 weeks later. In order to get continuity you should do one monthly sowing of about 5 plants for each sowing.

Spacing:
Between plants: 75cm
Between rows: 75cm

Romanesco broccoli

It produces lime green, conical shaped flower heads with an excellent flavour. Sometimes it is listed under the cauliflower section in seed catalogues.

Spacing:
Between plants: 75cm
Between rows: 75cm

"It may be tough to stomach at first, but it makes you stronger and healthier in the long run"

- Mark Vitner

Brussels Sprouts

Latin name:
Brassica oleracea Gemmifera Group
Family:
Brassicaceae (also known as
Cruciferae)
Related to:
Cauliflower, cabbage, broccoli,
radish, turnip, kale, swede, rocket,
cress, kohlrabi.
Botanical classification:
Brassica derives from the Celtic
bresic, the name for cabbage.
Oleracea means 'as a herb' – the
wild cabbage.

Introduction

Brussels sprouts are quite difficult
to grow organically. This is due to
mealy aphid attacks, especially during mild winter conditions. They
also occupy a fair amount of space
over a long period (8 months).
Hence, they are not a suitable crop
for a small garden.

Brussels sprouts are a very hardy
winter brassica. The sprouts are
botanically swollen buds. They
ripen on the bottom of the stalk
first.

Once ready the sprouts need to be
harvested regularly, otherwise the
sprouts will open up and become
unusable. It is one of the few
vegetables where I would only
choose a modern F1 Hybrid
because the sprouts stay closed for
a much longer period.

History

Brussels sprouts are one of the
most recently developed
vegetables. They were first
recorded in Belgium in 1750 and
reached England and France
around 1800.

Soil and site

Brussels sprouts are very hardy and
will grow on most sites. They
should be planted in very fertile
soil that has been well prepared
with compost or decomposed
manure. Brussels sprouts require a
firm soil for sprout production, so
the soil should be well settled

35

before planting. The ideal pH is 6.5 to 7.0.

Sowing

Brussels sprouts can be raised in a seed bed as bare root transplants or in modular trays. Personally, I prefer to raise them in modular trays and sow one seed per cell 2cm deep.

Early:
Sow under glass in mid March and transplant in late April.

Mid:
Sow under glass in early April and plant out in May.

Late:
Sow in early May and transplant in early June.

Spacing

Smaller types:
Between plants: 60cm
Between rows: 70cm
Tall types:
Between plants: 90cm
Between rows: 90cm

Rotation

It is absolutely essential to keep them in the brassica section of your rotation to prevent a build up of the numerous brassica pests or diseases.

Plant care

Brussels sprouts require a very firm ground, so ideally the soil should be prepared the previous autumn so it can settle. The transplants should be well watered before transplanting. They can be planted with a trowel or dibber. Regular hoeing will control weed growth as well as stimulating plant vigour. On exposed sites it is beneficial to earth up the soil around the stem to prevent wind damage. Some growers on very exposed sites tie the plants to sticks. However, I believe this is rarely necessary. Being a heavy feeder they would benefit from liquid feeds made out of nettle, comfrey and/or compost.

Stopping:
Stopping consists of removing the growing point from the plant which actually makes a lovely vegetable in its own right. Many commercial growers use this technique to speed up the development of the uppermost buds and to adjust the date of maturity. This technique is quite useless for a hobby gardener who is quite happy to harvest sprouts over a long period.

De-leafing:
Any discoloured leaves should be removed from the plant on a regular basis as they may harbour pests and diseases.

Harvesting

The harvesting period lasts for about 2 to 3 months. Start harvesting the lower sprouts first as soon as they are big enough. Remove the yellow leaves regularly as this makes subsequent harvesting easier and it may also keep the plants healthier as it increases air circulation and prevent sprouts from rotting.

Potential problems

Brussels sprouts are susceptible to the same pests and diseases as cabbage and the same control measures are recommended. However, mealy aphids are especially a problem with sprouts in particular.

How much to grow?

Each plant may yield about 2kg of sprouts so, if you have a large garden, 5 plants (5 m²) will give you many nice Sunday treats.

Varieties

Brigitte F1 (personal favourite, November to December harvest, excellent disease resistance and great flavour)
Igor F1 (early to mid-season type, fine flavour)
Rampart F1 (good disease resistance, good taste)
Wellington F1 (very winter hardy type, harvest from December until March)

Speciality type:

Rubine (red variety with excellent flavour)

"A fruit is a vegetable with looks and money. Plus, if you let fruit rot, it turns into wine, something brussels sprouts never do"
- P.J. O'Rourke

Cabbage

Latin name:
Brassica oleracea Capitata Group
Family:
Brassicaceae (also known as
Cruciferae)
Related to:
Cauliflower, Brussels sprouts,
broccoli, radish, turnip, kale,
swede, rocket, cress, kohlrabi.
Botanical classification:
Brassica derives from the Celtic
bresic, the name for cabbage.
Oleracea means 'as a herb' – the
wild cabbage. *Capitata* means
'having a head'.

Introduction
Cabbages are the most commonly
grown member of the brassica
family. They generally do
extremely well in our cool, moist
climate provided that plenty of
compost or ripened manure is
available. With good planning and
proper choice of varieties, it is
possible to have cabbages all year
round. Cabbages are tolerant of
freezing temperatures but less so
to excessive heat. The optimum
growing temperature is 15 – 18°C.

History
The English name cabbage comes
from the French *caboche,* meaning
head, referring to its round form.

Cabbage has been cultivated for
more than 4,000 years and
domesticated for over 2,500 years.
Although cabbage is often
connected to the Irish, the Celts
brought cabbage to Europe from
Asia around 600 BC. Since
cabbage grows well in cool
climates, yields large harvests and
stores well during winter, it soon
became a major crop in Ireland.

Legend and lore
Egyptian Pharaohs would eat large
quantities of cabbage before a
night of drinking, thinking the
consumption would allow them to
drink more alcoholic beverages
without feeling the effects.
Perhaps this is why many consider
cabbage with vinegar as a good
hangover remedy.

Soil and site

Cabbages are easy to grow and will tolerate most sites, even fairly exposed ones. Poorer soils can be improved by a fairly heavy application of half rotted manure or compost, ideally in the previous autumn, so that the soil can settle down. In the wetter areas it would be advisable to cover the beds with black plastic to prevent excessive leaching of nutrients. The pH level of the soil should be above 6.5, otherwise it should be corrected either in the form of calcified seaweed or ground limestone. An acid soil may encourage the spread of clubroot. Because cabbages are very demanding and greedy plants they have a negative effect on plants that take their place in the following year.

Sowing

Cabbages can be raised in a seed bed as bare root transplants or in modular trays.

I prefer sowing cabbages in modular seed trays which are placed in a greenhouse (or tunnel). I sow one or two seeds per module about 1.5cm deep. If two seeds germinate you have to remove the weaker seedling. They usually germinate within 5 to 7 days and are ready for planting out about 4 weeks after sowing.

Summer cabbage:
Sow from late March to mid April in a heated propagator at 15-18°C.
Autumn cabbage:
Sow from late April to early May.
Dutch cabbage (red and white):
Sow in late April.
Hardy winter cabbage and savoy cabbage:
Sow from mid May to early June.
Spring cabbage:
Sow from July to August.

Spacing

The spacing of the plants determines the size of the head. If lots of small cabbages are required plant them a little closer. If you want to impress your neighbours slightly increase the spacing. It is a common mistake to plant cabbages far too close.
Summer cabbage: 40-45cm
Autumn cabbage: 45cm
Dutch white & red cabbage: 45-60cm
Hardy winter cabbage: 45-60cm

Rotation

It is absolutely essential to keep cabbages in the brassica section of your rotation to prevent a build up of the numerous brassica pests and diseases.

Plant care

Cabbages require a firm ground. Ensure that the plants which were raised indoors are properly hardened off before planting out, especially early sowings. The transplants should be well watered before transplanting. They should be planted firmly with a trowel or dibber. Regular hoeing will control weed growth whilst stimulating plant vigour. Sow a few more than you need and then select the best for planting and keep some back for possible replanting.

Harvesting

With the help of the over-wintered cabbages and the spring cabbages it is possible to have cabbages throughout the whole year. The autumn and winter types keep extremely well in the garden and in store, whereas the spring and early summer cabbages have a much shorter cropping period. They need to be harvested once they are ready otherwise they will bolt or burst open. Some varieties are less liable to bolt (e.g. Stonehead F1).

Storing

If you choose a good selection of varieties you should be able to get cabbages fresh from your garden nearly all year round so there is no need to store them. The firm Dutch autumn cabbages store for a month or two in a cool shed.

Potential problems

Cabbages are susceptible to the same insect and disease pests as all the other brassicas, and the same control measures are recommended (see page 252).

How much to grow?

Cabbages take up a lot of space in the garden and are always very cheap to buy. You do, however get some satisfaction in growing a nice head of cabbage. This is only for joy and definitely not for saving money. There are plenty more high value and space efficient crops around.

Varieties

Spring cabbage:
Hispi F1 (pointed cabbage suitable for spring and summer use)
Pyramid F1 (dark green pointed variety suitable for autumn and spring planting)

Summer cabbage:
Stonehead F1 (excellent variety for summer to autumn use, very firm heads)
Minicole F1 (compact, slightly oval heads, ideal for smaller gardens)

Winter cabbage:
Tundra F1 (very hardy, professional variety with good taste)
January King (hardy variety with purple-tinged heads)
Celtic F1 (probably the best winter cabbage, very hardy, excellent taste)

Savoy cabbage:
Vertus F1 (very hardy, late maturing with greyish-green, well clustered leaves)

Dutch cabbage:
Rodynda (firm red heads, excellent flavour)
Dottenfelder Dauer (large firm heads which store well)

"Having a good wife and rich cabbage soup,
seek not other things"
- Russian Proverb

Calabrese

Latin name:
Brassica oleracea Italica Group
Family:
Brassicaceae (also known as
Cruciferae)
Related to:
Cauliflower, Brussels sprouts,
broccoli, radish, turnip, kale,
swede, rocket, cress, kohlrabi.
Botanical classification:
Brassica derives from the Celtic
bresic, the name for cabbage.
Oleracea means 'as a herb' – the
wild cabbage.

Introduction
What consumers call broccoli,
gardeners call calabrese. So if you
want to grow the broccoli from the
shops you have to buy calabrese
seeds. Sprouting broccoli has
either purple or white small
sprouts, whereas, calabrese has a
large green head.

History
Calabrese probably came from the
Eastern Mediterranean area in the
17th century.

Soil and site
Calabrese requires an open,
unshaded place. The soil should be
fertile, free-draining but with a
high water holding capacity. They
generally accept a slightly acid soil.
The soil should preferably have
been enriched with plenty of
farmyard manure the previous
autumn as their nitrogen
requirement is high.

Sowing
Calabrese can be sown in
succession from late March until
late June. I always sow calabrese
in modular trays which are placed
in a greenhouse. I sow one or two
seeds per module about 1.5cm
deep. If two seeds germinate you
have to remove the weaker
seedling. They usually germinate
within 5 to 7 days and are ready for
planting out about 4 weeks after
sowing.
For continuity I would sow a few
plants in late March, early May and
in early June.

Spacing

Spacing determines the size of the head produced. Wide spacing (45cm in rows 60cm apart) produces large central heads and numerous smaller side-shoots. Narrow spacing (10cm apart in rows 60cm apart) produces many terminal spears, which will be ready at the same time with no secondary side-shoot. Highest overall yield can be achieved by planting at a spacing of 15cm apart in rows 30cm apart. Calabrese should always have plenty of water. It benefits from a nettle feed (a good source of nitrogen) after the central head is cut in order to encourage shoot development.

Rotation

It is absolutely essential to keep calabrese in the brassica section of your rotation to prevent a build up of the numerous brassica pests and diseases.

Plant care

Calabrese requires plenty of water at all stages. Drying out results in smaller plants and premature budding so the heads remain small.

Harvesting

Cropping starts as early as June and may continue to the first frost. The central head should be cut before the flowers open. Smaller side shoots will develop later and one can expect 2 - 3 further cuts.

Generally cropping may start about 70 to 100 days after sowing depending on the variety and season.

Storing

Calabrese is best eaten fresh. However, if you have a glut the heads can be blanched and frozen.

Potential problems

Calabrese is susceptible to the same pests and diseases as cabbage and the same control measures are recommended (see page 252). The main problem with calabrese is premature flowering. It is absolutely crucial to check your plants for ripeness at least twice per week. The flower buds open up into yellow flowers so quickly and become useless.

How much to grow?

Three plants sown three times (see sowing dates) will be sufficient.

Varieties:

Fiesta F1 (reliable variety, good taste)
Marathon F1 (mid season variety, blue green heads, good disease and cold resistance)
Tiara F1 (very early variety, superb flavour)

Carrot

Latin name:
Daucus carota var. *sativus*
Family:
Umbelliferae (also known as *Apiaceae*)
Related to:
Parsnip, celery, celeriac, parsley, coriander, dill.
Botanical classification:
Daucus is the ancient Greek name for carrot. *Carota* means 'red rooted' and *sativus* means cultivated.

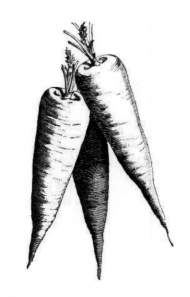

Introduction

Carrots derive from the wild carrot which is found throughout Europe and the British Isles. They are biennials, but are grown as annuals. If they are left in the ground they flower the following spring. Carrots are one of the richest sources of Vitamin A in human nutrition.

History

Carrots are native of Afghanistan where they were cultivated as early as 500 BC and then in the eastern Mediterranean region. Orange carrots were first developed in Holland in the 17th century. Before then carrots were either yellow, purple or red.
The Celts called them 'honey underground' due to their sweet flavour.

Types of carrots

1. **Berlicum** - large cylindrical stump rooted carrots.
2. **Chantenay** - medium broad short stump rooted, conical.
3. **Autumn King** - very large, long, slightly tapering. Good for storage and high yields.
4. **Nantes** - cylindrical, stump rooted. Used for early crops and forcing.
5. **Amsterdam** - small, slender, cylindrical, stump shaped root, excellent for forcing in tunnels.

6. **Round or stump-rooted** – they are useful for heavy or shallow soil and also for early cropping.

Soil and site

Early crops prefer a sheltered spot. Maincrop carrots thrive better on an open site. Carrots do best on light and stone free soil which is free-draining. The ideal soil pH is 5.8-7. However, carrots also do reasonably well on marginal soil, especially the stronger growing types like Chantenay and Autumn King. Under no circumstances add fresh manure to the soil before sowing. This will cause too much leafy growth at the expense of root development. The roots would also tend to fork trying to find the pockets of manure, rather than growing down. Forking of the roots also occurs if there are stones in the ground.

Well-rotted compost is best incorporated into the soil in the autumn and the soil should then be covered with black plastic over the winter to prevent leaching of nutrients.

Sowing

Carrots require a very fine seedbed and even under ideal conditions they germinate slowly (about 2 weeks). The stale seedbed technique should be used if possible. This involves preparing the seedbed and then leaving it for weeds to germinate. These should be hoed or raked before planting the carrots. This is even more effective if repeated twice prior to planting.

Seeds should be sown about 2cm deep in shallow drills and thinned to the required spacing. Weed control is essential in the early stages of growth to get the plants established.

Early carrots:
Early carrots can be sown from early April onwards. In cooler areas delay the sowing until the end of the month or even until May.

Maincrop carrots:
The most reliable sowing date for maincrop carrots is during the last week in May. This seems very late in the year, but a much more reliable crop of carrots can be grown this way.

This sowing will most likely avoid the first generation of the carrot root fly.

Spacing

Between plants: 3-4cm
Between rows: 20-25cm

Rotation

Carrots should be grown with the other members of the Umbellifer family. It is essential that carrots are rotated.

Plant care

Carrots should be kept well weeded at all times because they are bad competitors with weeds.

Harvesting

Early carrots can be pulled young and bunched as required with their leaves attached. Maincrop carrots should be harvested in the autumn before a heavy frost. On lighter soils they can be pulled by hand and the tops twisted or cut off. On heavier soil it is recommended to fork the roots out as they may otherwise break. In milder areas with very free draining soil one could consider leaving the carrots in the ground over the winter and harvested as required because the flavour is best when harvested fresh. In wetter parts the roots may rot.

Storing

Carrots are ideally stored in a box of moist sand in a cool frost free shed. Before storage, grading is essential. Any roots with carrot fly damage or diseases should not be stored with the healthy ones. They may keep until April.

Traditionally carrots were stored in clamps which can be made outside or under shelter. The carrots are piled up on a base of straw in a heap not more than 60cm high, then covered with a thick layer of straw and then a layer of earth (15cm thick). Unfortunately the wastage is generally quite high as mouse and rat control is difficult.

How much to grow?

If you eat 6 reasonable sized carrots per week, storing from October until the end of April (28 weeks) you will need 168 carrots.

If you space the seeds 4cm in the row and you fit 4 rows in a bed (bed width: 1.2m) you will get 100 carrots per metre.

In 2 metres you will get enough carrots from October to April.

Varieties

Amsterdam Forcing (early)
Autumn King (robust, heavy yielding variety)
Chantenay Red Cored (smooth skins, excellent flavour)
Nairobi F1 (early maincrop Nantes type with exceptionally high yields of uniform roots)
Narbonne F1 (maincrop Nantes type with good resistance to splitting)
Rocket F1 (I grew them the first time last year, already one of my new favourites)
Rothild (excellent German variety with very high vitamin content)
Speciality varieties:
Parmex (small, round carrots, very quick to mature)
Purple Haze F1 (bright purple carrots)
Rainbow F1 (a mix of white, yellow and orange carrots)

Potential problems

Symptoms	Probable cause	Comments
Carrots split	Sudden burst of growth. Wet spells after a dry period	Water during dry spells
Carrots twist around each other	Spacing is too close	Thin carrots to 3-5cm apart when the plants are small
Thin, spindly growth	Weed competition	Control weeds
Roots are forked or misshaped	Roots in contact with fresh manure. Compacted soil or stones. Overcrowding	Deep soil preparation. Remove stones. Thin early. Do not apply fresh manure
Carrots do not germinate	Old seed. Sown too deep or shallow. Soil crusted.	Maintain soil moisture until seedlings emerge. Check if seeds are viable.
Small tunnels on outside of root. Yellow or purple leaves.	Carrot root fly	See below
Roots rot, purple discoloration	Violet root rot, worse in wet soils	Grow in raised beds
Green tops on roots	Tops of roots exposed to sunlight	Cover exposed roots with soil

By far the most serious pest is the **Carrot Root Fly**. The flies' white little maggots bore tunnels in the outer layers of the carrot. This makes them very unattractive and susceptible to rot. It is impossible to eradicate as it feeds on a number of other umbelliferous vegetables and wild plants. There are, however, numerous ways of avoiding the carrot root fly:

- Sowing date:
Carrots which are sown in the first week in June generally avoid the first attack of the flies.

- Intercropping:
Many gardeners claim that intercropping carrots and onions discourages carrot fly and onion fly respectively by masking the scent of the vegetables. I have frequently tried this, but always unsuccessfully.

- Thinning:
The carrot flies are attracted by the scent of the carrots, which is released when the carrots are thinned and weeded. They travel far and fast so sow them correctly with the correct spacing. If you have to thin them do so as quickly as possible on a windy day and compost the thinnings.

- Barriers:
Putting a barrier about 60cm high of fine mesh around the carrot plot is a generally recommended practice. I think it is a myth and I don't believe it works.

- Crop covers:
The most successful control method is to cover the carrots with a crop cover such as bionet which is specially designed to keep out carrot root fly.

- Harvesting:
Maincrop carrots should all be harvested at the same time because during harvest the carrot flies are attracted in large numbers because of the smell. I always found if harvesting stretches over a few weeks the last ones are particularly infested with the maggots.

- Hygiene:
Ensure that all roots are harvested and trimmed leaves and infected carrots are taken away from the field and properly composted. Alternatively infected roots can be burned.

-Resistant varieties:
There are some varieties of carrots with some tolerance to carrot flies (Sytan, Resistafly and Fly Away).

"There are some oligarchs that make me want to bite them just as one crunches into a carrot"

\- Evita Peron

Cauliflower

Latin name:
Brassica oleracea Botrytis Group
Family:
Brassicaceae (also known as
Cruciferae)
Related to:
Brussels sprouts, kale, broccoli,
cabbage, swede, turnip, radish,
cress.
Botanical classification:
Brassica derives from the Celtic
bresic, the name for cabbage.
Oleracea means 'as a herb' – the
wild cabbage. *Botrytis* means 'like a
bunch of grapes'.

Introduction

Cauliflowers are one of the more
difficult vegetables to grow but
once you have tasted a home-
grown cauliflower all the effort will
seem worthwhile.

History

The oldest record of cauliflower
used as a food crop dates from the
6th century BC from Cyprus. It
was well developed in Syria in the
10th century.

Soil and site

Cauliflowers require a fertile, deep
soil with high moisture retention.
On the other hand the soil should
be free draining. The ideal pH is
6.5-7.0. Acid soils can lock up
essential trace elements and this
may cause defects such as whiptail
and tipburn.

Cauliflowers prefer cool growing
conditions. A temperature of 16-
18°C combined with a moderately
high humidity is ideal. Doesn't
this sound just like Ireland?

Sowing

I always sow cauliflower in
modular trays which are placed in a
greenhouse. I sow one or two
seeds per module about 1.5cm
deep. If two seeds germinate you
have to remove the weaker
seedling. They usually germinate
within 5 to 7 days and are ready for
planting out about 4 weeks after
sowing.

For continuity I would sow a few
plants in late March, early May and
early June.

Spacing

A spacing of 60cm x 60cm will produce decent sized curds. The spacing can be increased slightly if larger heads are required or decreased if smaller curds are preferred.

In the last few years there is a fashion for mini cauliflower. Some varieties can be spaced as close as 15cm x 25cm for that purpose.

Rotation

It is absolutely essential to keep cauliflower in the brassica section of your rotation to prevent a build up of the numerous brassica pests and diseases.

Plant care

Research has shown that yields can be greatly increased if the soil is kept moist at all times.

Harvesting and storing

If the cauliflowers are not harvested on time the curds (heads) will turn brown and rot.

It is important to give your plants the best growing conditions to build up their growth so that they can support a large curd.

When harvesting cauliflowers you should keep their leaf wrapping intact to protect the curd from damage.

Potential problems

Cauliflower is susceptible to the same pests and diseases as cabbage and the same control measures are recommended (see page 252).

Cauliflowers may also encounter other problems such as whiptail and tipburn.

Whiptail can be a problem on acidic soil where molybdenum is made unavailable to plants. The plants develop chlorosis (yellowing) between the leaf veins and in severe cases they may develop 'blind growth' (absence of growing point). Once the damage is seen it is too late to rescue the crop but liming the soil will help in future years.

Tipburn may also be a problem on acidic soils. The symptoms are brown margins on younger leaves and a discoloration of the curds. This is caused by calcium deficiency.

How much to grow?

To start off with, sow a few seeds at each sowing date as they all mature at the same time and do not store for more than a week.

Varieties

Andes F1 (an excellent, vigorous variety with excellent nutty taste)
Avalanche F1 (very productive medium sized type with tasty pure white curds)
Igloo F1 (vigorous growth and large snow white curds)

Speciality varieties:
Graffiti F1 (a truly novel variety with beautiful purple heads)
Minaret (small, lime green florets)
Purple Cape (hardy purple cauliflower)

Growing mini-cauliflowers

Growing mini-cauliflowers is a novel idea, especially suited to small families. The curds will only reach 7 to 10cm in diameter. For success with this novel crop you have to choose the right variety, grow at close spacing and make regular sowings.

Spacing:
A spacing of 20 x 20cm is ideal for mini-cauliflowers.

Regular sowings:
You should only sow a few plants for a small area at any one time and a continuous supply can be obtained by successional sowings as they will all mature at the same time. At a spacing of 20 x 20cm you will get 20 mini-cauliflowers per square metre.

Sowing dates:
Successional sowings can be made from mid April until mid June. Sow one seed per module.

Varieties
Igor F1
Alpha
Garant
Perfection

'Cauliflower is nothing but a cabbage with a college education'
-Mark Twain

Celeriac

Latin name:
Apium graveolens var. *rapaceum*
Family:
Umbelliferae (also known as *Apiaceae*)
Related to:
Carrots, parsnips, celery, parsley, dill, coriander.
Botanical classification:
'Apium' derives from the Celtic '*apon*' which means water; 'graveolens' means strong scented; 'rapaceum' means turnip like.

Introduction
Celeriac is an excellent winter vegetable which is a lot hardier than celery. It is grown for its edible swollen stem. Celeriac is closely related to celery. It is grown for its crisp, celery-flavoured root which really is a swollen stem. It can be eaten raw or cooked. It is a staple in Europe but little more than a novelty in Ireland.
Celeriac is not the easiest vegetable to grow due to its difficulty in raising it from seed but the one positive aspect is that it prefers to grow on moist conditions and dislikes heat.

Legend and lore
Apparently celeriac is a traditional remedy for skin disorders and rheumatism. It may also restore sexual potency after an illness.

History
Celeriac was developed from the same wild species as were our present improved varieties of celery, and at about the same time. It was first described by botanists in 1600. A hundred years later it was becoming more common in Europe, but was hardly known in England.

Soil and site
Celeriac likes a sheltered garden and a rich, loamy soil with plenty of well-rotted compost added to it. The pH should be between 6.5 and 7.0.

Sowing and planting

I raise them just like celery. But you have to do only one sowing in the third week in March. The transplants can be planted out after the last frost in late May/early June.

Broadcast the seeds into a standard seed tray or pot containing seed compost. The seeds should not be covered as they need light to germinate. The trays should be placed in a warm place either on a windowsill or in a propagator. Celeriac may take between two to three weeks to germinate. They can be pricked out into modular trays when the seedlings are 3cm tall (about 2 weeks after germination). It is really important that they are pricked out at an early stage otherwise there will be too much root disturbance which may lead to bolting at a later stage. Move the plants to the garden when the seedlings are about 10cm tall and harden off for at least a week before planting out.

Spacing

The highest yields can be achieved by a spacing of 35 x 35cm each way.

Rotation

Celeriac should be rotated along with other Umbellifers.

Plant care

Plants are shallow-rooted and require consistent moisture so be careful when hoeing because of their shallow roots. They will benefit from a top-dressing of well-decomposed compost or poultry pellets in the summer and water during dry spells. In summer remove the outer leaves to expose the crown and encourage the bulb to develop

Harvesting and storing

The roots can be harvested from October onwards. They can either be stored in boxes of sand or in mild districts they can be left in the ground and harvested as required.

Potential problems

The young plants need to be protected from slugs. The celery leaf miner (also known as the celery fly) may sometimes cause damage. The symptoms include blistering of the leaves. I don't think it's a common problem on celeriac. It generally is a very healthy and resistant vegetable.

How much to grow?

If you eat 2 celeriac per week, storing from October until March (24 weeks) you will need 48 celeriac.

If you space the plants 35cm apart in the row and fit 3 rows in a bed (bed width: 1.2m) you will get 9 celeriac per metre. In 5 metres you will get enough celeriac for 24 weeks.

Varieties

Balder (round roots with good flavour)
Brilliant (a new variety with well shaped large round roots, stores well)
Giant Prague (large root with good flavour)
Monarch (popular variety with a smooth skin and succulent flesh)
Prinz (excellent variety, smooth round roots)

"The greatest delight the fields and woods minister is the suggestion of an occult relation between man and vegetable. I am not alone and unacknowledged. They nod to me and I to them"
- Ralph Waldo Emerson

Celery

Latin name:
Apium graveolens L. var. *dulce*
Family:
Umbelliferae (also known as *Apiaceae*)
Related to:
Carrots, parsnips, celeriac, parsley, dill, coriander.
Botanical classification:
'Apium' derives from the Celtic *'apon'* which means water;
'graveolens' means strong scented;
'dulce means sweet, pleasant.

Introduction

Celery has become very popular in Ireland in recent years but unfortunately it is one of the most difficult vegetables to grow. It took me years to figure out how to grow good celery.
The secret of growing good celery is to sow it at the right time (not too early), choose a good variety (Lathom Blanching Galaxy or Victoria) and grow it on a fertile, moisture retentive soil with plenty of well-rotted compost added to it.

History

Celery is believed to be the same plant as selinon, mentioned in Homer's Odyssey about 850 BC. Our word 'celery' comes from the French celeri which is derived

from the ancient Greek word.
Wild celery grows in marshy areas in Europe, the Mediterranean, Asia Minor and the Caucasus. Celery has been used as an aphrodisiac.

The older types of celery required blanching of the stems in order to rid it of its unpleasantly strong flavour and green colour. This process involved digging a trench and planting the celery inside and gradually filling up the trench as the celery grew.
I have never come across anyone who grows celery in this way. I'm not even sure if these old varieties still exist.

Over the last few decades many so-called self-blanching varieties have appeared and made it much easier to grow celery.

No trenching or blanching is required.

Soil and site
Celery likes a sheltered garden. Too much exposure may cause the stems to become tough and stringy.

Celery prefers a rich, loamy soil with plenty of well-rotted compost added to it. The pH should be between 6.5 and 7.0. It can even tolerate soils that are less than well-drained because it was originally a wetland plant.

Sowing
Broadcast seed into a standard seed tray or pot containing seed compost. The tiny seeds should not be covered as they need light to germinate. The trays should be placed in a warm place either on a windowsill or in a propagator. The seeds may take between two to three weeks to germinate. The seedlings can be pricked out into modular trays when the seedlings are 3cm tall (about 2 weeks after germination). It is really important that they are pricked out at an early stage otherwise there will be too much root disturbance which may lead to bolting at a later stage. Move the plants to the garden when the seedlings are about 10cm tall and harden off for at least a week before planting out.

Seeds can be started about 10 to 12 weeks before the last frost. I usually start them off in late March for planting out in June.

Sowing dates for succession:
Late March
Late April
Late May

Spacing
The highest yields can be achieved by a spacing of 27 x 27cm each way. If you want smaller plants you can decrease the distance to 20 x 20cm or if you want to show off increase it to 35 x 35cm.

Rotation
Celery should be rotated along with the other Umbellifers.

Plant care
Plants are shallow-rooted and require consistent moisture. Lack of water will make the stalks fibrous and bitter. The plants should be kept weed free and moist at all times.

Harvesting
Celery can be harvested from mid summer until late autumn (if successional sowings were made). Harvest the whole plant when the stalks are reasonably big and before they get stringy. If you want to keep celery for a few days harvest early in the morning and trim the leaves off to leave about 25cm of stem and keep in a plastic bag in the fridge. They should keep for two weeks.

Potential problems

Celery may occasionally be attacked by the carrot root fly. The young plants also need to be protected from slugs. The celery leaf miner (also known as the celery fly) may sometimes cause damage. The symptoms include blistering of the leaves.

How much to grow?

Once mature, celery will only stand for 3 weeks in the garden, so only grow a few at a time.

Varieties

Celebrity (early maturing with crisp, nutty flavoured stems)
Lathom Blanching Galaxy (an excellent well flavoured and reliable variety)
Victoria F1 (excellent variety, great flavour, high quality and long standing ability)

Speciality varieties:

Giant Pink (hardy variety with pale pink stalks)
Solid Red (red stalked)
Standard Bearer (very hardy, red stalks)

"The thought of two thousand people crunching celery at the same time horrified me".
> - George Bernard Shaw
> (explaining why he had turned
> down an invitation to a
> vegetarian gala dinner)

Chicory

Latin name:
Cichorium intybus
Family:
Compositae (also known as
Asteraceae)
Related to:
Lettuce, endive, Jerusalem
artichoke, globe artichoke.
Botanical classification:
Cichorium is an ancient Arabic
name for chicory. *Intybus* is Latin
for Endive, the old name for
chicory.

Introduction
Chicory is a very popular vegetable
in Italy but is still very uncommon
in Ireland. This is due to its bitter
taste. I'm sure not many people
would like it. But you could
imagine it is an acquired taste. I
actually think it makes a delicious
salad. It is very easy to grow and is
more or less free of pests and
diseases.

History
Chicory is a native of Europe and
Asia. It is an ancient crop which
has been used by the ancient
Greeks and Romans.
The roots of chicory have long
been used as a coffee substitute.

Types of chicory
There are three types of chicory:
Forcing chicory
Red Chicory
Sugarloaf chicory

Forcing chicory:
The forcing or blanching of
chicory originates in Belgium
(1840) and the Belgians are still the
masters of producing this delicious
vegetable. To produce the
'chicons' (the name of the heads)
you sow a 'Witloof' chicory variety
in May in a bed. You should dig
out the long tap roots from
October until December. The

leaves should then be trimmed off about 2.5cm above the root.

The roots can be stored in boxes of sand until they are required for forcing. To force them, simply replant a few roots at a time in large pots (5l) with their necks about 2.5cm above the compost. After watering, cover the pot with another pot the same size but upside down and block all the drainage holes. At a temperature of 10-18°C they should form heads within 3 to 4 weeks. It is a very useful crop to have in winter.

Red chicory:

Red chicory is commonly known as 'radicchio'. Radicchio can be sown in modular trays from late May until early July. They do not tend to germinate as easy as lettuce so I usually sow two seeds in each module and thin to just one plant per module. They should be planted out at a spacing of 30 x 30 cm about 4 weeks after sowing.

Sugar loaf chicory:

This is one of my favourite vegetables but I have nearly given up promoting it as everybody to whom I gave a sample screwed up their faces in disgust. It is an easy vegetable to grow. The trick is not to sow it too early. The best time is between late May and early July. The autumn harvested crop can be stored for a couple of months if the plants are pulled with their roots and stored in a shed. The outer leaf may shrivel a bit but the inside of the heart will be perfect. It is extremely healthy, easy, pretty and to me: "delicious.' Why not try growing it?

Soil and site

Almost any fertile soil will produce good chicory. Apply well decomposed compost.

Sowing

Forcing or Witloof chicory:

Sow thinly in drills 30cm apart. Thin the plants to about 20cm apart in the row. Alternatively the seeds can be raised in modular trays (1 to 2 seeds per cell and thinned out to leave just one seedling) and planted out about 4 to 5 weeks later after hardening off. If they are raised in modular trays it is essential that the seedling are planted out at a young stage otherwise the taproot may become 'air-pruned and start to fork at a later stage.

Red chicory and sugar loaf:

Early sowings of chicory are often prone to bolting. The best time to sow chicory is from late May until early July.

The most successful method is sowing in modular trays. The seeds should be sown 1cm deep at a temperature of 15 to 18°C. I only sow one to two seeds per module and remove one of the doubles and transplant it to an empty space. You want to end up with only one seedling per module. The transplants are usually ready to plant out about 4 weeks after sowing and will be ready for harvesting after another 6 to 8 weeks.

In order to get continuity sow only small amounts in mid May, mid June and early July.

Spacing

There are so many types and varieties of chicory and they all require a different spacing. The best idea is to follow the recommendations on the seed packets.

Rotation

Chicory suffers from no specific pest or disease so you can use them anywhere in your garden wherever you have space in the summer.

Plant care

During dry weather the plants should be watered as dry soil will encourage bolting.

Harvesting and storing

The roots of the forcing 'Witloof' types can be stored in boxes of sand (layered) and forced as required throughout the winter.

The red radicchio types should be sown in succession as they do not keep well once harvested.

The sugar loaf chicory can be stored in a cool shed for a couple of months.

Potential problems

The only problems I have ever encountered with chicory are slugs and grey mould (botrytis) during wet weather.

How much to grow?

Just grow a few to see how you like them.

Varieties

Witloof chicory:
Brussels Witloof (one of the best known forcing types)
Zoom F1 (high quality chicons, easy to force)

Red chicory:
Cesare (an Italian variety for autumn harvest, very colourful)
Palla Rossa (delicate flavour, colour turn red when it gets colder)
Rossa di Treviso (crisp green leaves which turn red when cold)

Sugar loaf chicory:
Sugar Loaf (excellent winter variety, stores well)

Chinese Cabbage

Latin name:
Brassica rapa Pekinensis Group
Family:
Brassicaceae (also known as
Cruciferae)
Related to:
Cabbage, Brussels sprouts, kale,
cauliflower, radish, turnip, swede.
Botanical classification:
Brassica derives from the Celtic
bresic, the name for cabbage. *Rapa*
means 'of rape'.

Introduction
Chinese cabbage has become very
popular in continental Europe,
both for gardeners and consumers.
Unfortunately it seems completely
absent in Ireland. It is an
absolutely delicious vegetable and
very easy and quick to grow.

History
Chinese cabbage originated in
China and the earliest records date
from the fifth century AD. It is
believed to be a spontaneous cross
between pak choy and turnip. Only
in the 1970's did it become a
commercial crop in Europe.

Types
There are three types of Chinese
cabbage:

Cylindrical type:
It has a long erect leaves which
form a cylindrical head.
Barrel headed type:
It has a compact barrel shaped
dense head.
Loose headed type:
It produces leaves without forming
a head.

Soil and site
Chinese cabbage requires a deep,
fertile and well drained soil with
good water retention and a pH
range of 5.5 – 7. A generous
application of well decomposed
compost or manure is essential.

Sowing

Chinese cabbage is an excellent follow-on crop in summer. It can follow an early harvested crop such as early potatoes. In fact it is impossible to grow it in spring as it would bolt. Sowings in June and July produce the most reliable crops.

I generally sow 1 seed per cell into a modular tray. The plants are ready to transplant 3 to 4 weeks after sowing.

Spacing

The spacing for the heading type is 45 x 45cm.

Rotation

It is absolutely essential to keep Chinese cabbage in the brassica section of your rotation to prevent a build up of the numerous brassica pests and diseases.

Plant care

Chinese cabbage requires unchecked, rapid growth. To achieve this you may need to water during dry spells.

Harvesting
Heading types:

Harvest the mature heads when they are firm. The heads will keep for at least a month if placed in a plastic bag in the fridge.

Loose headed types:

It can either be harvested whole or individual leaves can be picked as a salad addition.

Potential problems

Chinese cabbage may suffer from the usual brassica pests and diseases. Fleabeetles are a particular problem with Chinese cabbage.

How much to grow?

I would recommend just to grow a few plants to find out how they perform in your garden and to see if you like them.

Varieties

I have tried growing the heading Chinese cabbage for years and have only been successful with the varieties "Yuki F1" and "Kasumi F1", both barrel headed types.

A reasonably good cylindrical type is "Jade Pagoda".

"How Love burns through the Putting in the Seed
On through the watching for that early birth
When, just as the soil tarnishes with weed,
The sturdy seedling with arched body comes
Shouldering its way and shedding the earth crumbs"
-Robert Frost

Courgette and Marrow

Latin name:
Cucurbita pepo
Family:
Cucurbitaceae
Related to:
Pumpkin, squash,
cucumber, melon.
Botanical classification:
From the Latin *cubirta*, a gourd.

Introduction
Courgettes are well suited to a small garden as they produce a very high yield from a small area. Two to three plants are sufficient to give you a fairly large amount of courgette during their season. Courgettes are the young immature fruits and when left to grow they turn into marrows.

There are special marrow varieties available but I doubt if there are too many dedicated marrow lovers around. And the trouble with courgettes is that they turn into marrows before you know it.

History
Courgettes originated in Mexico but now grow all over the world.

Soil and site
Courgettes need a fertile, free-

draining soil which can hold plenty of moisture. A generous application of well-decomposed compost is beneficial (about 1 bucket per square metre).
They also need a sheltered place in the garden as they really dislike strong wind (because of their large leaves).

Sowing
I usually sow seeds in late April individually into 7cm pots. Ideally, the pots are left in a propagator in the greenhouse or on a south-facing windowsill at home. They will also be fine in a tunnel without

a propagator but plants have to be covered up with fleece during cold spells to protect them from frost damage.

After about 3 weeks – or before the plants get potbound – I pot them on into 12cm pots which are still left in the greenhouse or indoors.

Planting

Start hardening off the plants at the end of May (see page 222) and plant out in early June. Do not plant if the weather forecast predicts cold windy spells which can be quite common during this time. In my first few years in Ireland I attempted to plant them out in May and they nearly always failed to survive. However, if you use cloches they should be fine.

Spacing

Please do not underestimate the space a courgette plant requires. The ideal planting distance is 1 metre. It is important to stick to this spacing but you can interplant some lettuce or annual spinach into the gaps. They can be harvested before the courgettes take over.

Rotation

Courgettes belong to the cucurbit family. This family is not prone to any soil borne pests and diseases, so you do not need to be too fussy with rotations.

Plant care

Apart from regular harvesting and keeping the weeds down there is very little else to do.

Below: Hand pollination:

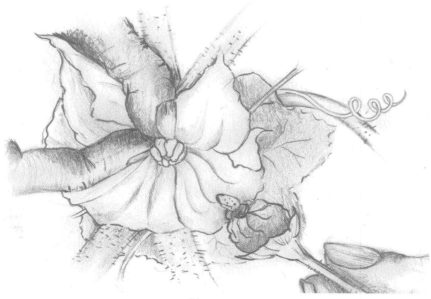

In cold, wet weather (when few insects are around) you can pollinate the flowers by hand. This will increase the chance to get fruits.

Courgette plants have separate male and female flowers. They are easily distinguished by looking at the flower stalk. The male stalk is plain and the female flower carries a small fruit on the stalk.
You transfer the pollen from the male to the female flowers with a soft brush or remove the male flower and rub it onto the open blooms of the female flowers.

Harvesting

Harvest courgettes as soon as they are the size you require. In fact, you may have to harvest them about 3 times per week. Overnight they could turn into monster marrows! Try to cut the fruit carefully with a sharp knife at the stalk without damaging the plant. It is best not to leave the marrows on the plants as this will sap all the energy from the plant and reduces the production of new fruits.

Storing

Courgettes do not store for more than a week in the fridge but marrows will last for about 3 months in a cool, but frost free building.

Potential problems

There are very few problems with courgettes. The main problem occurs if you plant them out too early. The plants will be damaged by strong, cold winds or die in the first light frost.
During the end of the season plants may get attacked by powdery mildew. There is no cure for it but it does not kill the plant.

How much to grow?

Do not plant too many plants. This year I planted three plants and my wife and children got seriously fed up with them. We had about 20 courgettes per week. Luckily our chickens loved them!

Varieties

Ambassador F1 (high yielding dark green fruits over a long period)
Defender F1 (very early, high yielding dark green fruits)
Parthenon F1 (all female, self fertile, ideal for early sowings)
Jemmer F1 (yellow variety with delicious nutty flavour)

"For all things produced in a garden, whether of salads or fruits,
a poor man will eat better that has one of his own,
than a rich man that has none"
- J.C.Loudoun

Endive

Latin name:
Cichorium endivia
Family:
Compositae (also known as *Asteraceae*)
Botanical classification:
Cichorium is an ancient Arabic name for chicory. *Endivia* means Endive.

Introduction
Endive is a very popular vegetable in Europe but is still quite uncommon in Ireland. Yet it is very easy to grow and is more or less free of pests and diseases.

History
Endive is an ancient crop which has been used by the Egyptians, Greeks and Romans. It was introduced to Central Europe in the 16th Century. The French used it as a medicinal plant 'to comfort the weake and feeble stomack'.

Types of endive
There are two types of endives: broad leafed and frisee types. I personally prefer the more attractive frisee types but the broad leafed varieties tend to be hardier.

Soil and site
Almost any fertile soil will produce good endive. Apply well-decomposed compost.

Sowing
Early sowings of endive are often prone to bolting. The best time to sow endive is from late May until mid July.
Endive is best sown in modular trays (1cm deep) at 18°C. I only sow one to two seeds per module and remove one of the doubles and transplant it to an empty space. You want to end up with only one seedling per module.
The transplants are usually ready to plant out about 4 weeks after sowing and will be ready for harvesting after another 4 to 6 weeks.

In order to get continuity sow only small amounts in modular trays in late May, early June and late June.

Spacing

Between plants: 25cm
Between rows: 30cm

Rotation

Endive suffers from no specific pest or disease so you can use them anywhere in your garden wherever you have space in summer. It is an excellent vegetable for intercropping.

Plant care

During dry weather the plants should be watered, as dry soil will encourage bolting.
Blanching (excluding light from the plants) reduces bitterness and makes the leaves more tender.
Some of the modern varieties do not necessarily require blanching. The recommended way for blanching is to pull the outer leaves together and tie with a string about 2 weeks before harvest and then place a plate over the whole head. I have never done it this way. I find it much easier to cover the whole plant with a bucket about 10 days before harvesting. Just cover a few plants at a time.

Harvesting and storing

Cut the whole heads when mature and blanched or use individual leaves from immature plants.

Once harvested, it should be consumed as soon as possible. Endive will keep in a plastic bag in the fridge for a week but only if it was harvested early in the morning when it is refreshed.

Potential problems

Apart from slugs, snails and aphids, endive is a very healthy crop.
Bolting often occurs if sown too early.

How much to grow?

In one square metre you get 12 plants.

Varieties

I prefer the curly leafed varieties such as:
Fine Maraichere (finely cut curled leaves)
Glory (finely serrated leaves on loose hearting heads)
Jeti (upright leaves, easy to blanch)
Pancalieri (self blanching type, frizzy leaves, rose tinted midrib)

Broad leaved types:
Avance (attractive, high yielding, cold tolerant)
Nuance (well filled hearts, excellent quality, resistant to tipburn)

"My salad days – when I was green in judgement"
-William Shakespeare

Florence fennel or bulb fennel

Latin name:
Foeniculum vulgare var. *azoricum*
Family:
Umbelliferae (also known as *Apiaceae*)
Related to:
Carrots, parsnips, dill, coriander, celery, celeriac.
Botanical classification:
Foeniculum derives from Latin for hay because of its odour. *Vulgare* means common.

Introduction
Florence fennel is closely related to the herb fennel. But unlike the herb fennel, Florence fennel is an annual and it is really a very delicate plant. It has very decorative feathery foliage and the base of the leaves form a white bulb just above ground level.
I am often surprised why garden designers never use Florence fennel in their borders.
It is also a delicious vegetable with a lovely texture and fresh taste – a hint of aniseed and celery.

History
Florence fennel was used by the Greeks and Romans who ate it in order to ward off obesity. The first records of it being grown in England date from the early 18th century. The bulb type was developed in Italy.

William Coles, in Nature's Paradise (1650) writes that 'both the seeds, leaves and root of our Garden Fennel are much used in drinks and broths for those that are grown fat, to abate their unwieldiness and cause them to grow more gaunt and lank.' It was also said to convey longevity and to give strength and courage.

Soil and site
Florence fennel grows well on any fertile, free-draining and moisture retentive soil with well

decomposed compost dug into it.
The ideal pH is 6.0 – 7.0.
The plot should receive full sun.

Sowing

Fennel does not like root disturbance, so I always sow them directly into modular trays (1-2 seeds per module) about 1cm deep and place the tray in a warm place (20° C). Thin out to one seedling as soon as seedlings are up. If the weather is poor or the soil temperature is too low I sometimes pot on the modules into 8cm pots and leave them in the tunnel. This delays planting out for a couple of weeks. It definitely produces better plants but it is more work and requires more tunnel space.

Sowing dates:

In order to get continuity sow only small amounts on the following dates:
Mid May: choose a bolt resistant variety such as Argo
Early June: Zefa Fino
Late June: Zefa Fino

Planting

Plant out modules about four to five weeks after sowing or pots about 7 weeks after sowing.
Especially the earlier crops need to be hardened off properly.

Spacing

A spacing of 35cm x 35cm will give you decent sized bulbs.

Rotation

Grow fennel in the Umbellifer (carrot) section of your garden.

Plant care

Keep the beds well hoed and weeded and water during dry spells as dry soil conditions may encourage bolting.

Harvesting

The bulbs should be ready about 3 to 4 months after sowing when the bulbs are about 7cm across. Cut the stalk below the bulb at ground level.
The bulbs will not keep very well. It is best to trim off all the leaves when you harvest. The leaves can be used for flavouring and stock. If the leaves remain on the harvested bulb they draw out the moisture and the bulb will become soft.

Storing

The bulbs may last for a few days if left in a plastic bag in the fridge.

Potential problems
Pests and diseases:

Slugs like the young plants and aphids feed on the leaves during warm dry weather.
If carrot root fly is a serious problem in your garden it may also affect fennel.

The most difficult problem is bolting. This happens especially if there is a period of cold weather after planting and also during dry spells.

In order to limit bolting you could delay sowing until early June, harden off transplants properly, water during dry spells and I recommend using a bolt resistant variety.

How much to grow?

Fennel is either adored or hated as a vegetable, so you can either grow lots or none at all.

Varieties

Zefa Fino (high quality, bolt resistant, solid bulbs)
Perfection
Romanesco (late variety with large round bulbs)
Rudy F1

"The fennel is beyond every other vegetable, delicious.
It greatly resembles in appearance the largest size celery, perfectly
white, and there is no vegetable equals it in flavour"
- Thomas Jefferson

Garlic

Latin name:
Allium sativum
Family:
Alliaceae (commonly known as
Alliums)
Related to:
Onion, scallions (spring onions),
shallots, leeks, chives.
Botanical classification:
Allium is the Latin term for garlic;
now the name of all the onion
family, or from Celtic *all*, meaning
pungent or burning. *Sativum* means
cultivated.

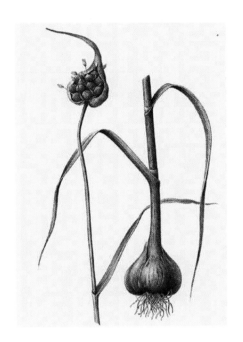

Introduction

Garlic is one of my favourite
vegetables. It is actually quite easy
to grow garlic and if you follow the
tips below you can grow good
garlic quite easily.
There are more than a hundred
different garlic varieties available
but garden centres often only stock
one or two types. Garlic can be
grouped into autumn and spring
planted garlic.

Here are a few tips on how to
grow great garlic:
- Increase the spacing between
plants to at least 20cm.
- Grow a good variety and plant

only first class bulbs (discard any
rubbish).
- Only buy bulbs from reputable
source, not just from a
greengrocer.
- If your soil is heavy, grow garlic
in raised beds.
- I found that autumn planted
garlic tends to be more successful
than the spring planted crop.

History

Garlic has a long history that
parallels that of the onion and leek.
The word "garlic" comes from the
Anglo-Saxon *garleac* (*gar*, meaning

"spear" or "lance," and *leac* meaning "leek").

The Egyptians put garlic into their tombs and fed it to their slaves who built their pyramids to ward off infections. The Greeks ate garlic before sporting events as a strengthener. The Romans disliked the strong flavour and odour of garlic but fed it to their labourers to make them strong and to their soldiers to make them courageous.

In medieval times garlic was hung outside to deter witches.

Soil and site

Garlic prefers a light, free draining soil. If the soil is heavy – make raised beds and incorporate well-decomposed compost. It is essential that garlic is grown in full sun.

Planting

Garlic is grown by planting individual cloves which are split off from the bulb. On average, there are around ten cloves per bulb. Ideally only guaranteed virus and nematode (eelworm) free cloves should be used, but I think one can use home saved garlic for a number of years provided they appear to be strong and healthy.

In order to get decent sized bulbs, plant the cloves 20 - 25cm apart each way. Most gardening books recommend a much closer spacing of 10 - 15cm. With this wider spacing the bulb size will increase.

The cloves are planted upright with the tips about 2cm below the surface. Only open the bulb prior to planting otherwise the cloves will dry up and be prone to disease.

Garlic generally requires a cold period of about 6 weeks at a temperature below 10°C. This is the reason why garlic has to be planted in autumn or very early spring. If it is planted too late individual cloves won't develop and you will be left with a solid, clove-less bulb.

Autumn planting:

I found this time of year most successful but only with a raised bed. Plant cloves outdoors from late September until early November and make sure you choose an autumn variety.

Spring planting:

Spring planting is more advisable if the ground is too wet in winter. However, the yield will be lower. Plant cloves outdoors from February until early April, making sure to choose a spring variety.

Spacing

Between plants: 20 - 25cm
Between rows: 25cm

Rotation

It is absolutely essential to rotate garlic. It can only return to the same plot after four years otherwise you may encounter a build up of soil borne diseases such as white rot. If you ever get white rot in your garden you will be unable to grow any alliums for the next ten years.

Plant care

Keep weed free. Garlic with its upright leaves is a lot more susceptible to weeds than broad-leafed plants.

Harvesting and storing

Garlic is ready to harvest when leaves turn yellow-brown. Unlike onions, harvest before the stalks fall over. This is important – otherwise the bulb opens up and it rots during storage.
Dig garlic out carefully with a fork. Remove excess dirt from the root but never cut off the foliage.
Garlic should ideally be dried in the sun for 3-4 weeks. As this is generally not possible in Ireland, dry in an airy open shed.

When the garlic is fully dried it can be tied into bunches.
If braiding, do so while tops still have moisture and are flexible. Rewetting of dry leaves is also possible but usually less satisfactory.
The longer the tops stay on, the longer the storage life.
Air movement is essential.
Store as cool and dry as possible. Relative humidity must be below 70% to prevent mould and/or root sprouting. The lower the temperature, the longer the storage life. Storage at high temperatures (e.g. room temperature) is satisfactory but for shorter periods.

Potential problems

Garlic is susceptible to the same diseases as onion but there are fewer insect problems.

Pests:

Garlic has very little pest problems. Its strong oil and natural chemicals actually repel pests. You can buy liquid garlic products for pest and disease control.

Diseases:

Garlic suffers from the same diseases as other members of the alliums. Thus it is absolutely essential to stick to a proper rotation. There is no cure – only prevention.

How much to grow?

You would possibly eat 1 garlic bulb per week. Garlic will store in a shed from September until the end of March (28 weeks) so you need a total of 28 bulbs.

So if you space them 20cm apart in the row and you fit 4 rows in a bed (bed width: 1.2m) you will get 20 garlic bulbs per metre.
In only 1.5 metres of your bed you can grow enough garlic to give you one bulb per week for 28 weeks!

Varieties

The best garlic I've ever grown came from the Garlic Farm in the Isle of Wight. They stock a wonderful range of both autumn and spring planted garlic and also mail it to Ireland.

Early Wight (produced on the Isle of Wight suitable for autumn planting, the earliest maturing garlic, purple skin)
Cristo (excellent variety for spring planting)
Messidrome (white skinned variety for autumn planting)
Printanor (suitable for spring planting)
Solent Wight (another excellent variety from the Isle of Wight, matures late, stores very well)

Unusual variety

Elephant garlic (*Allium ampeloprasum*): It is actually a form of leek even if it forms cloves that resemble garlic, but the appearance and flavour resemble leeks.

"What garlic is to food, insanity is to art"
Augustus Saint-Gaudens

Kale or Borecole

Latin name:
Brassica oleracea Acephala Group
Family:
Brassicaceae (also known as
Cruciferae)
Related to:
Cabbage, Brussels sprouts,
kohlrabi, cauliflower, radish,
turnip, swede.
Botanical classification:
Brassica derives from the Celtic
bresic, the name for cabbage.
Oleracea means 'as a herb' – the
wild cabbage. *Acephala* means
'without a head'.

Introduction

Kale is one of the hardiest winter vegetables and one of the easiest to grow. It seems to be much less plagued by all the brassica pests and diseases. I just wish we could like it more. Some varieties of kale, such as Redbor F1 and Nero di Toscana, are so attractive looking that they would deserve a prime place in your flower garden.

History

The kale is the most similar plant to the wild ancestor of so many cultivated brassicas – *Brassica oleracea* – which still grows wild on the western coasts of Europe.
It was already grown in Roman times.

Soil and site

Kale prefers a fertile, deep soil with high moisture retention. The soil should be free draining and kale will tolerate poorer soils than most brassicas. The ideal pH is 6.5-7.0.

Sowing

Kale can either be raised in a seed bed as bare root transplants or in modular trays. If raised in modular trays it is essential that they are planted out before they become pot bound. I find that modular grown plants establish much easier. I sow one seed per cell 2cm deep.
Sow early varieties in mid April until early June.

Spacing

Between plants: 60cm
Between rows: 50cm

Rotation

It is absolutely essential to keep kale in the brassica section of your rotation to prevent a build up of the numerous brassica pests and diseases.

Plant care

Apart from keeping the soil well hoed and weeded you should remove any discoloured lower leaves from the plant to improve the air-flow through the crop and thus minimise pests (aphids) and diseases (moulds).

Harvesting and storing

Kale is such a forgiving plant. You could neglect it for months and still get many dinners out of it. You should start harvesting the bottom leaves first. You can take a good few each time but you should always leave the top 8 leaves to grow on.

Potential problems

Kale is the easiest and healthiest brassica you can grow. It will suffer from all the common brassica problems but generally to a much lesser extent.

How much to grow?

If you eat kale regularly three plants are sufficient, if you want them for the occasional meal 1 or 2 plants will do.

Varieties

Darkibor F1 (tightly curled, dark green leaves)
Nero de Toscana (also known as Black Tuscany, dark green palm like leaves)
Pentland Brig (very hardy, old established variety, leaves not curly)
Redbor F1 (most attractive looking kale with curly purple leaves)
Red Russian (blue green kale with purple tinges on the leaves)
Ripbor F1 (very high yielding and very hardy)

Speciality type

Jersey Tree Kale (also known as Walking Stick Cabbage; can grow up to 3m tall)

"Kale is a leafy vegetable that is bold and bitter but it's packed with vitamins and minerals. You can juice it like you would carrots, putting whole stalks into a vegetable drink. It'll boost your greens and your energy levels"
-Chi Lang

Kohlrabi

Latin name:
Brassica oleracea Gongylodes Group
Family:
Brassicaceae (also known as
Cruciferae)
Related to:
Cabbage, Brussesls sprouts, kale,
cauliflower, radish, turnip, swede.
Botanical classification:
Brassica derives from the Celtic
bresic, the name for cabbage.
Oleracea means 'as a herb' – the
wild cabbage.

Introduction

The common name derives from
the German – *Kohl* meaning
cabbage and *rabi* meaning turnip.
In this type of cabbage the stem
remains very short and swells just
above ground level to form an
edible corm.
Kohlrabi is one of my favourite
vegetables to grow.
Unfortunately only a minority of
gardeners in Ireland have ever
attempted to grow this beautiful as
well as unusual vegetable and
probably even fewer people have
ever eaten it.
So why not try it? It is one of the
easiest brassicas to grow and it
tastes a bit like a turnip, except a
lot better. The best quality is
obtained with rapid, unchecked
growth which is provided by mild
temperature and a constant supply
of moisture and nutrients.

It is described as a brassica with a
ball-shaped stem. It comes in three
colours – white, purple and green.

History

Kohlrabi originated in northern
Europe in the 15th century.

Soil and site

Kohlrabi requires an open,
unshaded place. The soil should be
reasonably fertile, free-draining and
with a high water holding
capacity.

Sowing

I always sow kohlrabi in modular trays which are placed in a greenhouse or tunnel. I sow one or two seeds per module about 1.5cm deep. If two seeds germinate you have to remove the weaker seedling. They usually germinate within 5 to 7 days and are ready for planting out about 4 weeks after sowing.

In order to get continuity, sow only small amounts in mid April, mid May, early June and late June.

Spacing

A spacing of 30 x 30cm will give you decent sized kohlrabi. If you prefer smaller vegetables you can space them 20cm apart in the row and 30cm between the rows.

Rotation

It is absolutely essential to keep kohlrabi in the brassica section of your rotation to prevent a build up of the numerous brassica pests and diseases.

Plant care

Caution: When planting out kohlrabi, do not plant it deeper than it was in the module and never earth up the plants as they grow. These are techniques used for other members of the Brassica family. With kohlrabi the bottom of the bulbous stem would rot.

Harvesting

Harvest when the bulbous stems reach at least tennis ball size. Many gardeners believe that they get tough if left to grow bigger. I do not necessarily agree with this. Spacing determines the size and if the plants grow steadily even a large kohlrabi will taste quite tender.

Storing

Kohlrabi does not store well so should be harvested as needed.

Potential problems

Apart from the usual brassica problems, kohlrabi may suffer from the following disorders.

Bolting:

The main problem with kohlrabi is that it is likely to bolt if the temperature drops below 10°C for two to three days. This can be avoided by not sowing too early.

Woodiness:

Sometimes kohlrabi may become woody and thus quite unpleasant to eat. This is always caused when the plant growth slows down or if the plants are getting too old.

To prevent woodiness, simply provide the plants with ideal growing conditions: adequate water supply, soil fertility and not sowing too early.

How much to grow?

One metre of a bed will provide you with 15 kohlrabi plants.

Varieties

Azur Star (very early variety with attractive blue bulbs)
Logo (white variety with good resistance to bolting)
Patrick F1 (green variety suitable for growing in summer)
Purple Danube (an excellent, high-yielding blue-purple variety)
Superschmelz (a traditional German variety which is quite different than
the others. It can grow to an enormous size and still be very tender and
unlike the others it can be stored throughout the winter)

"In all things of nature there is something marvellous"
-Aristotle

Leek

Latin name:
Allium porrum, or *ampeloprasum*
Family:
Alliaceae (commonly known as
Alliums)
Related to:
Onion, garlic, chives, scallions,
shallots.
Botanical classification:
Allium is the Latin term for garlic;
now the name of all the onion
family, or from Celtic *all*, meaning
'pungent' or 'burning'. *Porrum*
derives from the Celtic *pori*, to eat.

Introduction

The leek is a popular winter
vegetable. It is one of the few
fresh vegetables from your garden
during the cold months. It is easy
to grow and is of very high value.
It is a biennial plant grown for its
long white shanks (stems). Leek
varieties differ in the colour of
their leaves, their hardiness and in
the degree of bulbing at the stem
base. Generally those with blue or
purplish green leaves are hardier.

History

Archeologists have found remains
of leeks in Egyptian tombs dating
back to 1550 BC. The wild
forefather of the leek still grows in
southern Europe from Portugal,
north Africa, Turkey and Iran.
Leeks originate from southern
Europe & northern Africa from
the wild species *Allium
ampeloprasum* and were distributed
by the Romans across Europe.
It became a national plant of the
Welsh people early in their history.
Tradition has it that the Welshmen
led by their King Cadwallder in
AD 640 in a victory over the
Saxons, adorned their hats with
leeks grown in nearby gardens in
order to distinguish themselves
from the enemy warriors.

Legend and lore

The Emperor Nero is reported to
have been nicknamed Porrophagus
because of his inordinate appetite
for leeks. He imagined that

80

frequent eating of leeks improved his singing voice!

Soil and site

Leeks prefer an open site with deep fertile loamy soil enriched with plenty of farmyard manure or compost. Leeks are heavy feeders and respond well to compost or manure applications. The ideal pH range is between 6.5 - 7.5.

Sowing

There are three ways of sowing leeks:

1. Seedbeds:

Traditionally leeks were sown into outdoors seedbeds and then transplanted into their final position about 10 weeks later when pencil thick.

2. Modular trays:

This is my preferred method. I sow two seeds per cell and about 6 to 8 weeks later plant them out in twos. The cells are not split up. The plants are ready to transplant when the seed compost is held together by the roots and will not fall off. When double planted the spacing is also doubled, instead of 15cm apart in the row, they are planted 30cm apart.

3. Deep seed trays:

Another excellent way is to sow the seeds into polystyrene fishboxes which are about 15cm deep. You fill the boxes with seed compost and make shallow drills about 7cm apart and sow the leek seeds into the drills about 2cm apart and then cover up the drills.

Sowing dates

From just three sowing dates you can get fresh leeks from your garden from July until April:
- Sow summer and autumn varieties in modular trays in mid February in a propagator and plant out in mid April.
- Sow autumn and winter varieties in modular trays in mid March in a propagator and plant out in mid May.
- Sow a late winter variety in modular trays in early May and plant out in early June.

Planting

Leeks can be planted around 6 to 8 weeks after sowing in modular trays or 10 weeks if grown in an outdoor seedbed. The modules can be planted when the roots hold the compost together in the cells. Bare root transplants should be pencil thick before transplant-ing. Leeks are generally planted in holes made by a dibber and watered in or firmed in using the dibber as a lever. I find the dibbing technique quite unsuited to heavy soils. I have frequently seen dibber holes with struggling leek plants and their roots exposed to the air dangling around in it. The reason was that the dibber sealed off the edges of the hole and the leeks could not grow through it. But why torture the poor little plants anyway? Just plant them like any other vegetable (but still deep) and cover up the roots.

Many gardening books still recommend to trim off the roots and leaf tips before planting out but research has shown that this lowers the yield.

Spacing

Between plants: 15cm (or 30cm if two plants are planted together)
Between rows: 30cm

Rotation

It is essential to adhere to a strict rotation with leeks. They should be rotated along with the other alliums.

Plant care

As the plants grow earth up the leeks with soil to blanch the stems. This simply means the covered part of the leek turns white. Be careful that you don't get soil into the heart of the leek. Generally, I earth them up twice during the growing season.

Harvesting

Early varieties may be ready in late summer to late autumn. Late varieties are very hardy and can be harvested right through the winter until spring.

Potential problems

Leeks are relatively trouble free. Rust is however an increasingly common problem. When affected by rust, orange patches of spores appear on leaf surfaces. Some modern varieties are more resistant to rust. Rust may slightly reduce the yield and can make the plant look unattractive but it won't kill the plant. The good news is that rust itself is killed by a sharp frost. Leeks may also suffer from the general allium diseases such as white rot, but they are really a lot more resistant than onions.

How much to grow?

You would possibly eat two reasonable sized leeks per week. You can get leeks from your garden from August until March (32 weeks) so you need 64 leeks. So if you space them 15cm apart in the row and you fit 3 rows in a bed (bed width: 1.2m) you will get 18 leeks per metre. In only 3.5 metres of your bed you can grow enough leeks for 32 weeks!

Varieties

Varieties with erect foliage may be more suitable for organic growing. There is more ventilation through the crop and this may help in preventing rust and leaf blotch.
Summer types:
Roxton F1 (an excellent high quality leek with dark green erect

leaves, very high yielding, harvest from July until September)
Autumn types:
Autumn Mammoth Hannibal
Winter types:
Bluegreen Winter (a very hardy leek with blue-green leaves, harvest from December until March)
Shelton F1(an excellent high yielding variety)
Oarsman F1 (late maturing variety with excellent vigour and uniformity)
Late winter types:
Blue Solaise

"Eat leeks in March and wild garlic in May
And all year round physicians may play"
- Old Welsh Rhyme

Lettuce

Latin name:

Lactuca sativa

Family:

Compositae

Related to:

Endive, chicory, Jerusalem artichokes, globe artichokes, cardoon, sunflowers.

Botanical classification:

Both its common and its Latin name are based on an easily noticeable characteristic - it has a heavy, milky juice when cut. This juice is highly narcotic. The word 'lettuce' is derived from the Old French laitues (plural of laitue), meaning 'milky', referring to this plant. The Latin root word *lac* ('milk') appears in the Latin name *lactuca*.

Introduction

Lettuce is without doubt the world's most popular salad plant. By careful selection of varieties and successional sowing (sow little and harvest often) you can fresh lettuce for at least six months of the year.

History

In 2000 BC it was used in Egypt as an edible medicinal herb, as well as for oil production from its seeds.

In Greek mythology the young Adonis was killed by a wild boar in a garden of lettuces where he had hidden much to the despair of his lover, the goddess Aphrodite.

In the Roman epoch, lettuce was well established. It was held on high esteem by the Romans for its cooling and refreshing properties. The Emperor Augustus attributed his recovery from a dangerous illness to it, built an altar to it, and erected a statue in its honour. Lettuce has been an important part of human diets since ancient times. It was customary for the Romans to precede their gargantuan banquets with refreshing lettuce salads in the belief that lettuce enhanced the appetite and relaxed the alimentary canal. It had other uses too. Dried lettuce juice was used to aid sleep in Elizabethan times and through

World War II lactucarium, a sedative made from wild lettuce extracts, was used in hospitals.

Hippocrates, the Greek philosopher, describes the healing qualities of lettuce. He was born in Cos (from where the lettuce takes its name) in 456 BC.
The bitter milky juice has also been used as a substitute for opium in medicine.

Types of Lettuce
Butterhead:
Butterheads were the only commonly known lettuce in Ireland for a long time. They form a heart with soft, delicate leaves. They have the reputation of being quite bland tasting, but some varieties of butterhead and, especially if organically grown, can taste quite nice. Butterhead types are not suitable for the cut and come again system.

Crisphead:
Crispheads (or Iceberg) have become very popular in Ireland in the last twenty years or more. They form a large firm, crisp and succulent heart. Again their reputation for blandness makes them unattractive for home gardeners. However, if organically grown, and choosing the right variety, they can make an excellent salad.

Cos:
The Cos lettuce forms a dark green, upright, elongated heart. The leaves are long, crisp and sweet. To my mind they are the tastiest lettuces available.
Some varieties of Cos, however, are susceptible to a disorder called tipburn during the summer months (see potential problems).
The smaller relative, Little Gem, is the most popular type.

Loose leaf:
These lettuces do not form hearts thus making them suitable for picking individual leaves as required. They mature quickly and are very easy to grow. There are hundreds of varieties, which include Lollo Rossa and Bionda, Red and Green Salad Bowl.

Batavia:
Batavia lettuces are a fairly new introduction to Ireland. They are a cross between butterhead and crisphead lettuce. Most varieties are attractive looking and very tasty with lovely crunchy leaves.

Stem lettuce (Celtuce):
The name celtuce derives from Celery and Lettuce (CELery-letTUCE). It is grown for its edible stem which can reach up to 80cm. The heart of the stem has a delicious nutty cucumber–like flavour. Celtuce is a very popular vegetable in Asia, but is virtually unknown in Ireland. Seeds are available from a few seed companies and it can be grown quite easily here.

Note:
Many people believe that rocket, mizuna, mustards or cresses

belong to the lettuce family. This is not the case. It is important to remember that they are in the brassica family and should be grown in the brassica section of the rotation.

Soil and site

Any reasonable garden soil will do for lettuce. Half a bucket of well-rotted garden compost per square metre is sufficient. I advise not to use fresh or semi-decomposed manure for lettuce as it makes the plants grow too fast and they will become more vulnerable to pests and diseases. Lettuce requires a pH of 6.5-7.5.

Sowing

Important: Many lettuce varieties fail to germinate when the soil (or compost) temperature is above 25°C. This is important to remember because these temperatures often occur even in spring and summer if your plants are raised in trays in a tunnel. During hot spells move the trays into a cool shed for 2 days and then back into the tunnel. At 18°C lettuce will germinate after 3-4 days.

I generally sow lettuce seeds in modular trays. If I want a head of lettuce, only one seed per cell is required. For cut and come again lettuce I generally sow 3-5 seeds per cell. Lettuce needs light to germinate, so do not cover the seeds with compost. In most areas

in Ireland seeds can be sown from early April until July. In milder areas in the country you can try to extend the season slightly. If you have a polytunnel or greenhouse the season for lettuce growing can be vastly expanded (9-10 months of the year).

Timing:
From sowing to planting out: 3-5 weeks depending on the season and the weather.
From planting to harvesting: 4-6 weeks.

Planting

When planting out lettuce which has been raised in a greenhouse or windowsill it is absolutely crucial to harden the seedlings off before planting out.

Spacing

Small lettuce (Little Gem)
Between plants: 20cm
Between rows: 20cm

Medium lettuce (Lollo types, butterheads etc)
Between plants: 25cm
Between rows: 25cm

Large lettuce (Iceberg)
Between plants: 35cm
Between rows: 35cm

The seedlings should be planted with their seed leaves (cotyledons) just above ground level (see diagram next page).

If your seedlings do get a bit leggy you can safely plant them a little bit deeper in order to cover the stem but only up to the seed leaves. The plants definitely seem to appreciate this extra care.

But never plant the seedling deeper. If the growth point of the plant is buried it will rot away.

Rotation

Lettuce is an ideal plant for filling gaps in your vegetable plot e.g. plant between widely spaced crops such as kale and can be harvested before the kale needs that space. If you have any spare space anywhere in your garden you can happily plant lettuce there. Take note not to plant lettuce in the same spot the following year to prevent a build up of pests and diseases

Plant care

It is important to keep your lettuces weed free at all times and avoid spilling earth onto the leaves while weeding. During dry spells you may have to water the plants.

Harvesting and storing

I think, with lettuce, you will often have the same problem: it is either a feast or a famine. They nearly always ripen at the same time and quickly go into flower.

You can pick leaves from the leafy lettuces as soon as they are of a usable size. You can also cut loose leaf lettuce about 5cm above the base of the lettuce and it will send out new leaves which can be cut again about 2 to 3 weeks later.

Correct planting depth:

Tip:
Harvest lettuce at sunrise!
It is really true: the earlier in the day you harvest your lettuce the longer it keeps and the more nutritious it is. If you harvest lettuce at 6am and put them in a plastic bag in the fridge it will keep for a week as fresh as when harvested. If you harvest lettuce on a sunny day at 2pm it is already wilted as water has evaporated from the leaves and the sunnier the day the more water evaporates.

Potential problems
Pests:

Leatherjackets
Leatherjackets are the larvae of the cranefly (daddy longlegs). These are the louts of your vegetable patch as they just eat through the stem of newly planted lettuce moving along the row leaving a trail of destruction. They eat the stem of newly planted lettuce. It is important to check your newly planted seedlings regularly and inspect the soil under each destroyed lettuce and pick up the larvae before it moves onto the next plant. You can then replant the empty space with a spare lettuce. They are abundant in grassland so anybody with a new garden is sure to encounter them.

Cutworms
Cutworms are the larvae of some moth species. They do similar damage as the leatherjackets but are less common.

Slugs and snails
Everybody knows that lettuce is one of the favourite slug gourmet dishes. Apart from the general tips on slug control and prevention, ensure that your lettuce seedlings are properly hardened off before planting. It might be a good idea to spread organic slug pellets (Ferramol) around the plants.

Leaf aphids
Every year you will get a spell when aphids suck out the juice of your lettuce. Most of the time, the damage is not severe and you can simply rinse them off.

Root aphids
I have noticed in various gardens that root aphids are becoming an increasing nuisance. You notice them when you pull up a sick looking lettuce plant and you find white powdery dust with small white aphids all around the roots. Once you have it, there is no cure for this lettuce. To prevent further outbreaks, try the following combination of methods:
- Do not grow lettuce in affected areas for a couple of years.
- Do not plant lettuce after lettuce.
- Use tolerant varieties.
- Do not leave your plants in the ground for too long. As soon as a lettuce is ready, harvest it and pull out the roots.

Diseases:

The two most common diseases in lettuce are downy mildew (Bremia) and grey mould (Botrytis).

There are now many Bremia-resistant varieties available and grey mould can be avoided if they are grown in a clean weed free garden.

Disorders:

Tip burn

Tip burn is a physiological disorder associated with a lack of calcium, especially if the soil is too dry. This is the brown discolouration on the tip of the leaves rotting the plant eventually. There is no cure for it, but luckily there are now many varieties which are resistant to tipburn.

Leggy seedlings

Lettuce seedlings are prone to become leggy. The reason is generally lack of light. So make sure that your propagation area is in full sun. In Ireland we get plenty of natural shade..

Leggy seedlings are weaker and the plants are thus more prone to pests and diseases.

How much to grow?

Most people sow too many seeds at one go and have a massive glut at some point and nothing afterwards. From one sowing they will all ripen around the same time and will only last for a week or two in the garden before they bolt (go to seed).

A little bit of planning will provide you with lettuce for many months. For example if you eat 5 heads of lettuce per week sow 15 seeds every fortnight. The 5 extras are spares for potential slug or leather jacket casualties.

Varieties

Butterhead

Buttercrunch (a cross between a butterhead and a crisphead, with a crunchy heart and soft outer leaves)

Dynamite (an excellent uniform variety with aphid resistance)

Marvel of four seasons (very attractive red-green variety, very popular)

Matilda (fast growing and aphid resistant variety)

Loose leaf

Crosby (a much improved lollo bionda type with excellent disease resistance)

Aruba (a red salad bowl type with an excellent colour and compact habit)

Catalogna Cerbiatta (a highly ornamental oak leaf variety with deeply lobed leaves)

Fristina (very curly leaves and an excellent crisp texture)

Nika (a much improved lollo rossa type, with frilled red leaves, very good disease resistance)

Crisphead (or Iceberg)

Brandon (high quality variety with excellent mildew resistance, produces large dense heads)

Dublin (a reliable variety with

round solid heads)
Iceberg (very large crisp white hearts)
Lakeland (forms tight heads even in poor summers)
Saladin (an excellent and reliable variety)

Cos
Chatsworth (one of the sweetest tasting lettuce, with bubbly textured pale green leaves)
Little Gem Delight (an improved Little Gem type produces compact heads with a sweet nutty taste)
Pinokkio (dark green medium sized cos lettuce with crisp hearts)
Rusty (unusual large dark red cos)
Seville (very attractive red cos)
Sherwood

Batavia
Campania (light green colour and open, but well filled hearts; tolerant to tip burn)
Roger (fast growing reddish brown batavia lettuce with crunchy leaves)

"Lettuce is like conversation. It must be fresh and crisp, and so sparkling that you scarcely notice the bitterness in it"
- C.D. Warner

$\mathcal{O}ca$

Latin Name:
Oxalis tuberosa
Family:
Oxalidaceae
Related to:
No other vegetable

Introduction
Even if you don't fancy eating this delicious vegetable it deserves a good place in your ornamental garden as a beautiful curiosity. It resembles the native wood sorrel (also an Oxalis) and develops lovely yellow flowers in late Autumn.Oca is an amazing crop, but unfortunately it still remains virtually unknown outside of the Andes mountains.

History
Ocas are the second most widely grown root crop for millions of traditional highlanders in the Andes. It has been cultivated there since ancient times. The Incas have developed many diverse varieties.

Potential
While the potato has spread and become one of the world's most important food crop, oca, despite being good tasting, nutritious and high yielding, is still little grown outside the region. Most importantly it never gets blight as it is not in the potato family. I have grown oca here in Leitrim for many years and never had any problems with pests and diseases. Researchers believe it is one of the 21st centuries most promising new crops as it has the potential to be grown in a wide range of climate zones: Himalaya, northern China, Africa, Central America, New Zealand, Japan and Europe.

Soil and site
Oca thrives at altitudes too high for most other crops and yields well in poor soils. It is are also very successfully grown in New Zealand at sea level. A light rich soil with a pH between 5.7 and 7.5 is favoured.

The tubers begin to form only after the days are shorter than 9 hours. A long autumn season is important for good yields. It would be very beneficial to protect the plants from frost for as long as possible.

Sowing

Ocas are grown just like potatoes. Tubers can be planted in late April. In some years I plant the tubers in 10cm pots in April and leave them in tunnel, then harden them off in May and plant out at the end of the month.

Spacing

Between plants: 30cm
Between rows: 40cm

Rotation

Oca does not need to follow a strict rotation as it has no specific pests or diseases.

Plant care

It is beneficial to earth up the stalks just like with potatoes.

Harvesting and storing

Ocas should not be harvested before the end of October. I usually wait until the first frost has killed off the leaves as they grow right up to the end of the season. Ocas may be stored for several months in boxes of sand in a cool frost-free shed.

Potential problems

There are really no pests or diseases which trouble ocas. Isn't that great, especially with all the worries we have with the potato?

How much to grow?

As the tubers are difficult and very expensive to obtain I would start growing just a few to see if you like them. Each planted tuber will yield up to 15 tubers in the autumn. You should save the best ones for replanting the following year.

Varieties

In the Andes there are many different types of oca. However, they don't have English variety names. They come in different shapes and sizes. The colours range from yellow, red, purple to almost black. We only have the yellow and red type here.

Onion

Latin name:
Allium cepa
Family:
Alliaceae (commonly known as alliums)
Related to:
Garlic, leeks, shallots, chives, scallions.
Botanical classification:
Allium is the Latin term for garlic; now the name of all the onion family, or from Celtic *all*, meaning pungent or burning. *Cepa* derives from the Celtic *cep*, a head.

Introduction

Onions are amongst the most versatile of vegetables. They are easy to grow and are one of the few vegetables that can be planted early in spring when your gardening itch starts. They are also very productive – from a relatively small area you can get enough onions to last for half the year. In my opinion, onions are an essential ingredient in any garden and indeed in any dish.

History

Onions are one of the oldest vegetables known to mankind. There is clear evidence that they originated in Afghanistan, Pakistan and Iran. It was an important part of the diet in Egypt between 2800 to 2300 BC and were included in their religious festivities.

Onions were one of the crops that the Israelites bewailed that they could no longer get when they started their trek to the Promised Land. The Greeks and Romans are thought to have acquired the plant through their contact with Egypt and from that point, onions spread across Europe.

Legend and lore

Gerarde, in *The Greate Herbal* (1596) stated:
"The juice of onions snuffed up into the nose purgeth the head . . . stamped with salt, rue and honey . . . they are good against the biting of a mad dog . . . annointed upon a bald head in the sun bringeth the haire again very speedily."

Types of onions

There are two types of bulb onions – spring and autumn types (Japanese onion). Either of them can be grown from seed or planted as sets (small immature onion).

The spring planted crops are the most commonly known, but I think the autumn planted Japanese types are also worth a try especially if you have free draining soil.

You can use the Japanese onions from June onwards and eat them until the spring crop will be ready by late July. The spring crop will store well into late winter if you manage to dry them well.

Onions have brown, yellow, white, red or purple skins and also come in different shapes.

Soil and site

Onions require a reasonably fertile soil with a good tilth and excellent drainage. If you have a heavy, wet soil it is essential that you make a raised bed to avoid potential disease problems. They should not receive fresh or semi-decomposed manure. A dressing of well-decomposed garden compost is beneficial. The ideal pH for onions is 6.5-7.5 so you may have to apply ground limestone or even better calcified seaweed. Onions prefer an open, sunny site.

Sowing and planting
Growing from sets:

Growing onions from sets is a lot easier for a beginner. Onion sets are small immature onions. You simply plant the little bulbs around mid March-mid April in a well prepared, firm seed bed. The red varieties are safer to be planted in April as they have a greater tendency to bolt and a later planting may reduce the likelihood of this.

The Japanese onions are planted in September to early October.

The general recommendation is to plant them so that the top half of the bulb is still showing above ground. In areas where birds like to play with them (or mistake them for some insect) and pull them out, you could plant them a little bit deeper with the tips just showing above ground.

At home I have to protect them from the birds with a cloche for the first month until they have rooted properly.

The disadvantage of sets is that the choice of variety is very limited; you generally get just one red and one brown variety.

Essential tips for choosing sets:

Onion sets should be firm, rounded, no shoots or roots visible and of small to medium size.

It is quite simple: the better the sets the better your crop will be. I would recommend you buy them in a garden centre which sells them loose. I would never buy the small pre-packs as I usually throw more than half of them away. From a big sack pick out only the best ones (see diagram on page 99). Apparently the very big sets are more likely to bolt.

Growing from seed:

If you grow onions from seed you have a wonderful choice of varieties but it takes a lot longer and you need a greenhouse and a heating bench to start them off. Some gardeners believe that onions grown from seed are healthier and less likely to bolt. I found this to be true in some years but not in others.

The most reliable way of sowing onions from seed is to start them off in late January to late February. I usually sow 4 seeds per cell in a modular tray and place the tray on a heating bench in a greenhouse or polytunnel. Around mid-March I move the tray off the heating bench but still leave it in the tunnel. In early April start hardening off and in late April they can be planted out. I plant each module containing the four seedlings (do not split them up) into the garden.

Spacing
Seeds:

Modular grown seedlings (4 seeds per module) are spaced 30x30cm apart each way and staggered.

Sets:

The highest overall yield form sets can be achieved by a spacing of 25cm between rows and 7cm in the row. This close spacing, however, only produces small onions unless your soil is very fertile. I always space them 10cm in the row.

If you want to impress your neighbours simply plant them 15cm apart in the row and you will get enormous onions but the yield per square metre will drop significantly.

You can also plant four sets close together in a block and space each block 30cm apart each way like the modular grown seedlings.

Rotation

It is absolutely essential to rotate onions in order to minimise various soil borne diseases such as white rot.

Plant care

Apart from regular hoeing and weeding there is little else to do. Be careful, however, that you do not hoe too deep as onions have a very shallow root system. You may be better off hand weeding at the later stages. Some gardeners even eliminate this by planting the sets through black plastic. I have never been a fan of this technique. I suppose I like hoeing too much.

Harvesting

The overwintered onions can be used from June onwards as required. You should aim to use them up before the spring planted crop is ready as they do not store well.

Spring planted onions are excellent for storing throughout the winter. Unfortunately, Ireland tends to have the least favourite climate to dry onions before storage. These onions should be pulled in August when around 75% of all leaves turn yellow and fall over.

The bending over of the stems in order to encourage ripening is still a popular tradition. However, research showed that this practice increases storage diseases.

In some years, especially wet ones, they stay green for too long. In that case you could try to accelerate the ripening process by pulling the bulbs a little bit to break off some roots. About 10 days later you should pull them out completely.

The best way to dry the bulbs would be to leave them on the beds, ideally not touching each other, in full sun. The Irish weather conditions unfortunately make this impossible. So, ideally pull the onions on a sunny day and leave them outside until the first rains, then move them into an open shed and lay them on chicken wire or pallets in a single layer. You want to keep the rain off but still have good air circulation. You should also remove excess soil around the roots but do not remove the skins.

Storing

Once dry they can be tied in bunches (plaits) and hung in a dry, frost free shed or even in the kitchen.
If the onions are properly dried they will keep until March the following year.

Important:

Never cut off the stalks of your onions before they have dried otherwise they will rot within a few weeks. If you want to store them loose wait till the stalks are papery and pull off easily. This is possible about 2 months after pulling.

Potential problems
Pests:

The onion fly and onion eelworm are the most commonly known pests. The onion fly lays its eggs at the base of the bulb, the plant turns yellow and dies prematurely. When you look at the bulb you will find white maggots inside.

Eelworms are tiny creatures that live in the soil and affect the bulb by distorting them. The population can be minimised by a strict crop rotation in which no member of the onion family is grown on the same piece of ground for at least four years. Apparently weeds such as chickweed, bindweed and may-weed are also hosts of this eelworm. If you have an eelworm problem in your garden ensure that you eliminate those weeds. Maybe I am lucky, but I have never come across any of these two pests.

Birds love newly planted onion sets. They either think it is something nice to eat and get disappointed and scatter them all around the place or they may be looking for nesting materials.
To overcome this problem either put up a cloche with bird-netting or enviromesh or plant your sets just blow ground level.

Diseases:
Onion diseases are more likely to cause you grief than pests. They include white rot, neck rot and downy mildew.

White rot is the most serious disease on onions as the spores will last for more than seven years in the ground. Stick to a proper rotation with the onion family because if you have it in your garden you may never be able to grow onions again for many years. The symptoms of white rot include stunted plants with yellow and wilted leaves and if you pull an onion up you will find white mould on the base.
Neck rot only develops during storage. The onions may look quite healthy in the garden but develop a grey mould on the neck when in storage. Thus it is quite important to check your stored onions regularly and discard any rotten ones. This occurs when the bulbs have not been fully dried. Neck rot can also be caused by overfeeding – especially with fresh manure.

Downy mildew is a very common disease in Ireland. The disease thrives in cool wet conditions. The symptoms start at the tips of the leaves which become pale and die back and the disease moves down towards the bulbs. In some years I lost a lot of onions because of that. As there is no cure, the only chance we have is to prevent it as much as possible. Apart from praying for a good summer you can try a combination of the following:
- Grow your onions in a raised bed to improve drainage.
- Keep them weed free at all times to improve air circulation around the plants.
- Space them slightly further apart (12cm in the row).
- If you can choose grow them on a more open site (better air flow).
- Do not overfeed them as this causes soft tissues which are more susceptible to the disease.
- Never water them (excess water would spread the disease faster).
- Intercrop onions with other small leafed vegetables such as carrots to

slow the spread from one plant to the other.

Other problems
Bolting:
Bolting is a very common problem with onions especially the red varieties. There is little you can do to stop it. Bolting is usually caused by weather conditions, a cold spring followed by a hot summer.

Methods to reduce the risk of bolting:
- Slightly delay planting if it is very cold in March. Sow in early April. This is especially recommended for red onions which are more susceptible to bolting.
- Research has shown that smaller sets are less likely to bolt than bigger sets.
- There are different opinions whether seed sown onions or sets are more liable to bolt.
- Create a firm seedbed for the onion sets either by firming it down by standing on a plank of timber or by preparing the seedbed a month earlier and let it settle. In loose soil the plant roots do not seem to get hold of the soil and the plant thinks it is starving and reacts by going to seed.

How much to grow?
If you eat 5 onions per week, storing from September until the end of March (28 weeks) you will need 140 onions.
If you space the seeds 10cm in the row and you fit 4 rows in a bed (bed width: 1.2m) you will get 40 onions per metre.
In 3.5 metres you will get enough onions from September until March.

Varieties
The choice of varieties available as sets is very limited. My favourite ones are Centurion, Sturon and Red Baron, but as mentioned earlier the first priority is the quality of the sets, rather than the variety.
If you grow onions from seed you have a much better choice of variety. Recommended varieties:
Ailsa Craig (a very old variety and still renowned for its fine quality and flavour)
Kelsae (the real massive exhibition onion with an excellent flavour)
Red Baron (an attractive red skinned variety with a unique flavour)
Setton (developed from Sturon but with a rounder shape)
Sherpa F1 (high yielding variety with good tolerance to downy mildew)
Snowball (a superb white variety with mild flavour, stores well)

Other types of onions
- Welsh Onion
- Potato Onion
- Tree or Egyptian Onion

These old rarities are available from specialist catalogues and the Irish Seed Savers Association.

Diagram below illustrates the ideal onion set:

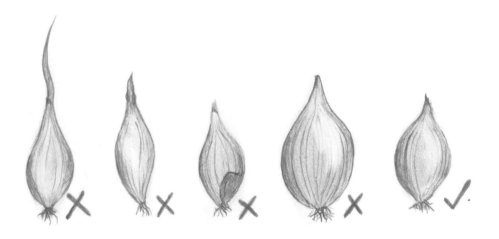

"An onion can make people cry but there's never been a vegetable that can make people laugh"
- Will Rogers

Oriental Salads

Introduction

Oriental salads have become very fashionable in recent years. There is a massive range of different types with different colour texture and taste available. Most of them are in the brassica family with a few exceptions. Some of them are quite hot and spicy. You can try growing them all year round, but they are at their best from late summer until winter as they are very hardy. The spring sowing tend to bolt very quickly.

My favourite types:
Brassica salads:

Mibuna (similar in taste to Mizuna but with long narrow leaves)

Mizuna (very popular salad leaf, very hardy and fast growing)

Mustard 'Golden Streaks' (pale green leaves with stunning serrated leaves, very fast maturing)

Mustard 'Red Frills' (like golden Streaks but with an amazing red colour, it will brighten up and salad bowl)

Mustard 'Green in the snow' (one of the hardiest salads, but beware: it tastes just like mustard. I love it!)

Komatsuna (often used as a salad leaf but traditionally cooked like spinach in Japan)

Pak Choi 'Joi Choi F1' (probably the best pak choi variety with dark green leaves and pure white leaf stem)

Rocket, Salad (distinctive tasting leaves which are deeply lobed)

Rocket, Wild (smaller serrated leaves with strong flavour; perennial plant)

Tatsoi (excellent variety with small, round, dark green leaves with crispy stem)

Non brassica salads:

Corn salad (lovely winter salad with distinctive nutty flavour)

Claytonia or winter purslane

(without doubt one of the best winter salads, you'll find your children nibbling away at the crop)

Soil and site

Any moderately fertile and moisture-retentive soil is suitable, preferably in a sheltered position.

Sowing

Oriental salads grows best in the cooler parts of the year. As the days get longer the plants quickly run to seed.

Seeds can be sown directly in early spring as soon as the soil can be worked or even in late summer or early autumn. The plants are quite hardy and can cope with a few degrees of frost. Because plants are quite short-lived, sow in succession of about two to three weeks.

Seeds can also be sown in modules (4 seeds per cell) and later transplanted. It is important that the seedlings never get stressed (through irregular watering or being pot bound) as this will definitely cause the plants to bolt.

Spacing

Between rows: 25cm
Between plants: 20cm (4 plants per station)

Rotation

The members of the brassica family need to be rotated with the other brassicas.

It is essential to keep the plot completely weed free otherwise you may get some weeds in your salad bowl. I appreciate that many weeds taste quite delicious but there is the odd horrible or even poisonous one. Keep the plot moist at all times to slow down bolting.

Harvesting

You can either harvest individual leaves as they are needed or use the cut-and-come-again method: cut the whole plant at about 5cm height from the soil level and the leaves will re-grow within the next two to three weeks. The leaves get bitter when the plant starts to bolt.

Potential problems

Flea beetles are the worst enemy of the oriental brassica salads but they do not affect the non brassica salads. They are tiny jumping beetles which eat hundreds of little round holes into the leaves especially in the spring. You may find that you can't grow them in spring or early summer in your garden unless you protect them throughout their entire life with a fleece or bionet. The late summer and autumn sowings should be safer.

*"To make a good salad is to be a brilliant diplomatist – the problem
is entirely the same in both cases. To know
exactly how much oil one must put with one's vinegar"*
— Oscar Wilde

Parsnip

Latin name:
Pastinaca sativa
Family:
Umbelliferae (also known as
Apiaceae)
Related to:
Carrot, celery, celeriac, parsley,
coriander, dill, chervil.
Botanical classification:
From the Latin *pastus*, 'food'. *Sativa*
means 'cultivated'.

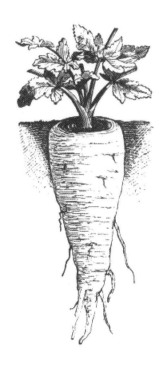

Introduction
I am delighted that parsnip is still a
very popular vegetable in Ireland.
It is a very hardy and reliable
vegetable to grow. I love the
distinct sweet flavour. It requires a
long growing season. In fact, the
flavour is greatly enhanced by cold
temperatures.

History
Parsnip is an ancient vegetable
which originated around the
eastern Mediterranean. The
Greeks and Romans called both
the carrot and parsnip *'pastinaca'*.

During the Middle Ages parsnips
were valued for their medicinal
properties; for treating problems
such as toothache, swollen testicles
and stomach ache. During the
16th century, parsnip cultivation
was widespread and became a

staple for poor people in Europe.
Parsnips were used as a sweetener
until sugar beet was developed in
the 19th century and apparently, a
parsnip beer was made in Ireland.

Site and soil
Parsnips prefer an open, sunny
site. Deep sandy soils are ideal but
even in heavy soils (especially if
dug over deeply) excellent results
can be achieved.
Parsnips prefer well decomposed
compost. The ideal pH is 6.5-7.

Sowing

It is important to remember that parsnip seed only lasts for one year.

The traditional sowing date for parsnips is in early spring. It says on the back of seed packet to sow between February and March. I can guarantee that you will have absolutely no success if you stick to that.

The best time to sow parsnips is in May. It is very simple: the warmer the soil, the quicker and better they germinate. I have even found April to be a difficult month for sowing parsnips in Ireland. If you sow in May the seeds will germinate far quicker and more evenly but the parsnips will also suffer much less from the most common parsnip disease 'canker'.

Parsnips require a very fine seedbed and even under ideal conditions they germinate slowly (about 2 weeks). The stale seedbed technique should be used if possible: this involves preparing the seedbed early in the year and then leaving it for weeds to germinate. The weeds should be hoed or raked before planting the parsnips. This is even more effective if repeated twice prior to planting thus eliminating many weeds before the crop is sown.

I always sow seeds directly into the ground. They should be sown very thinly (about 5cm apart) in rows 30cm apart and about 2cm deep. Parsnip seeds are quite big so they can easily be spaced out accurately. They are, however, very papery and light, so choose a calm day for sowing. As soon as they have all germinated you can start thinning them out.

Spacing

The final spacing will determine the size of the root:

10cm spacing produces small roots, 15cm spacing produces medium sized roots, 20cm spacing produces large roots.

If you forget to thin them the parsnips will be no bigger than a pencil. You may wonder why not sow them at their final spacing so we do not have to thin them at all? The reason is that not all seeds will germinate and you may want to allow for the occasional slug casualty.

Rotation

Parsnips should be rotated with the other members of the Umbellifer family.

Plant care

There is very little maintenance apart from thinning and weeding the crop.

Harvesting and storing

The parsnips are ready from October onwards. They are best left in the ground and harvested fresh as required. Parsnips get a better flavour if they are exposed to frost. This changes the stored starch into sugar and makes them sweeter.

If, however, your soil becomes waterlogged it is better to dig them all out and store them in boxes of sand in a cool, frost free shed. They will keep until the following April.

Potential problems

Parsnip canker
Canker is a very common problem with parsnips. I think you will always get a little bit. The symptoms are orange brown spots starting at the shoulder of the root. The canker organism also causes silvery-brown leaf spots.

Control:
- Select disease resistant varieties such as 'Gladiator' or 'Tender and True.'
- Improve drainage.
- Carefully observe rotation.
- Delay sowing until May.
- Earth up parsnips in summer to prevent spores reaching the roots.
- Increase soil pH to 6.5 to 7.

Carrot root fly
It can affect parsnips as well but generally to a lesser extent than carrots are affected. For control methods see carrot section.

How much to grow?
If you eat 3 reasonable sized parsnips per week, storing from October until the end of March (24 weeks) you will need 72 parsnips.

If you space the seeds 15cm in the row and you fit 3 rows in a bed (bed width: 1.2m) you will get 20 parsnips per metre.

In 3.5 metres you will get enough parsnips from October to March.

Varieties
Javelin F1 (my favourite variety, very high quality smooth tapering roots, some canker resistance)
White Gem (broad shoulders and white skin, highly resistant to canker)
Gladiator F1 (vigorous roots with a fine flavour, good resistance to canker)

"For ...... we can make
liquor to sweeten our lips
Of pumpkins and parsnips and
walnut-tree chips"
- Henry David Thoreau

Pea

Latin name:
Pisum sativum
Family:
Leguminosae
Related to:
Runner beans, French beans, broad beans, clovers.
Botanical classification:
Pisum is the classical Latin name for pea, probably derived from the Celtic *pis*, meaning pea.

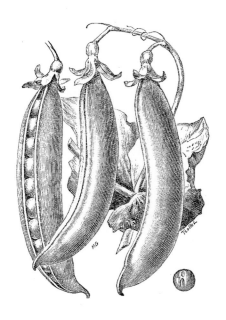

Introduction

If you try to get your children interested in vegetable growing, this is the crop to grow. They are so easy to sow and grow. Children love to eat them raw. On the negative side they need a fair amount of attention with regards to training; they are prone to pests and diseases and produce only a relatively small yield for the space they occupy. But all this is worth it for the flavour of a freshly picked garden pea.

History

The earliest record of peas date from 7,000 BC in the Mediterranean region. The ancient Greeks and Romans loved peas and grew them in abundance. The Romans are credited with introducing peas to northern Europe. Until the 16th century, peas were eaten dried and ground. The fresh garden peas only became popular in the 17th century.

Types of peas

There are three types of peas:
- Garden pea (or podding pea)
- Mangetout pea
- Sugar snap pea

The garden pea is the traditional pea, the one you take the seeds out of the pod. Within this group there are round and wrinkled seeded types, dwarf and tall types, some with coloured flowers and pods and semi-leafless types which have edible tendrils.

The mangetout types are eaten whole when the pods are still flat. The shells are usually quite thin.

The sugar snap peas are also eaten whole when the pods have swollen (like a normal garden pea) and the shells are usually quite fleshy.

Soil and site

Peas require a sunny and sheltered site. They grow best in a fertile and free draining soil. Good drainage is very important for early crops as the seeds would rot in cold and wet soils.

Sowing

Make sure you know what type you are growing (garden pea, sugar snap or mange-tout), and label the rows clearly. Otherwise they are easily confused and you do not know at which stage to harvest them.

Garden peas can be sown in small pots or in guttering pipes indoors for planting out later. I really think there is absolutely no need for that. The seeds are so easy to handle and they germinate so reliably, that I always sow peas directly outdoors in drills 4cm deep and 10cm wide. Sow them 5cm apart in the drill.

You can grow them in a single drill in the middle of the bed and support them with a fence or in a double row 70cm apart and erect a bamboo/branches framework.

I usually make two sowings, one in early April if the soil and weather conditions are reasonable, otherwise delay it. The second sowing is done in late May to June.

Spacing

Between plants: 5cm
Between rows: 70cm (if you have a double row)

Rotation

Peas are in the legume family and should be rotated along with them.

Plant care

Dwarf peas need little climbing support. If they are grown in closely spaced double rows they may hold each other up together. Any stragglers could be helped with a short branch.

The tall pea varieties need to be trained up adequately. This can be done with sticks, chicken or sheep fence or bamboo canes.
Peas, however, find it difficult to climb up bamboo canes, so you should use twigs in between the canes.
Remember to check the height of the variety you grow and erect a high enough frame for the peas.

Harvesting

Peas can be harvested from June until September. The pods should be picked regularly (once or twice a week), so they are still tender. If you do not harvest regularly and allow the plants to ripen the seeds, they will soon stop flowering. So even if you are completely fed up with them they should still be picked if you want your crop to continue.

Storing

Peas are best eaten fresh. If you have too many, you can blanch and freeze them for the winter months.

Potential problems

Mice can be a big problem, especially when they find the newly planted delicious seeds. The main disease is powdery mildew. The leaves and pods develop a sticky grey-white substance. Peas will probably always develop this disease in the late summer but if you grow the variety Greenshaft you will have much less of a problem. With good cultural practices (rotation, good healthy fertile soil, healthy seeds and resistant varieties) these problems can be overcome.

How much to grow?

A 4m bed of peas will yield about 4 to 6 kg of peas.

Varieties

Garden Peas:
Hurst Greenshaft (the one and only!)

Mangetout:
Carouby de Maussane (very tall, purple flowers)
Delikata (very productive, resistance to mildew, 60-75cm tall)
Oregon Sugar Pod (tall growing mangetout pea with excellent flavour)
Sugar Dwarf Sweet Green (dwarf pea, 60cm tall, suitable for early sowings)

Sugar Snap:
Sugar Ann (produces high yields of stringless sugar snaps, height 75cm)
Sugar Snap (very sweet, round podded, up to 1.8m tall)
Zucolla (excellent dwarf sugar snap pea with high yields, good mildew resistance, 75cm)

Speciality Pea:
Ezeta's Kromber Blauschokker (very unusual tall growing pea with distinctive purple pods)

"We lived very simply- but with all the essentials of life well understood and provided for – hot baths, cold champagne, new peas and old brandy"
- William Manchester

Potato

Latin name:
Solanum tuberosum
Family:
Solanaceae (Nightshade Family)
Related to:
Pepper, tomato, aubergine, tobacco, nightshades.
Botanical classification:
Solanum is the name given by Pliny, the Roman naturalist, to one of the nightshades; possibly derived from the Latin *solamen*, a solace, from its medicinal virtues. *Tuberosum* means tuber-bearing.

Introduction

The potato really is the national vegetable of Ireland. The curious thing about it is that the potato was only introduced to this country relatively recently. It was one of the many exotic plants brought back to Europe from South America by explorers during the sixteenth century. Cultivation spread rapidly throughout Europe as potatoes provided an ideal crop for peasant farmers with smallholdings.

By growing potatoes, a small area of land could provide enough nutrition to provide a basic subsistence diet for a family. It soon became the staple food of much of the population.

In Ireland the potato rapidly became the main item in the diet of the poorer people. With this new food source providing a healthy basic diet the rural population rose rapidly. As potatoes could grow on poor soils, the areas under cultivation expanded and even today the outline of old potato ridges can be seen high up on mountainsides especially in the West of Ireland.

The potato is the world's fourth most important food crop after wheat, maize and rice. It is also the most important root crop. It certainly has been the most important crop in Ireland since the

17th century.

History

The potato was first cultivated in Chile and Peru 5000 BC.

1563: Introduction to England from Spain by Sir John Hawkins.

1586: Second introduction to Ireland by Sir Francis Drake.

1725 onwards: potato became staple crop for the poor in Ireland.

1740: First potato famine due to severe frosts that destroyed the potato crop.

1821: Second potato famine due to extreme wet autumn. The crop rotted in the ground.

1842: Potato blight arrived in Europe (first in Germany and then Belgium).

1845: Blight arrived in Ireland.

1846: Blight destroyed the entire potato crop in Ireland.

1879: Another failed potato crop.

Late 1880's: Discovery of Bordeaux mixture to control blight.

Table:
Area under potatoes in Ireland

Year	Potato Area
1847	115,000 ha
1848	328,000 ha
1865	431,000 ha
1900	265,000 ha
1930	195,000 ha
1961	117,000 ha
1980	57,000 ha
1996	33,000 ha

Legend and lore

The potato caused division between Catholics and Protestants in the mid-1700s. Suspicious of this 'devil vegetable', which had to be buried like a corpse before it would grow, the Protestants even brought the fight to politics - in 1765 their slogan was:

'No potatoes. No Popery'.

From Grime's Herbal:

'To carry a raw potato in the pocket was an old-fashioned remedy against rheumatism.

Ladies in former times had special bags or pockets made in their dresses in which to carry a raw potato for the purpose of avoiding rheumatism if pre-disposed thereto.'

'The Potato Diggers' Song' by Thomas C. Irwin (1848)

For we must toil this autumn day,
With heaven's help, till rise of the moon.
Thanks God, and nothing my boy, remains
But to pile the potatoes safe on the flure,
Before the coming November rains,
The peasant's mine is his harvest still;
So, now, my lads, let's work with a will
Work hand and foot
Work spade and hand;
Work spade and hand
Through the crumbly mould.
The blessed fruit
That grows at the root
Is the real gold
Of Ireland.

Did you know?
The word 'spud' came from a tool which was used to weed the potato fields.

Irish Folklore:
People used to burn the potato skins in the fire as they believed they cleared the chimney of soot.

Types of potatoes
Potatoes are classified according to their time of maturity:
- First early
- Second early
- Early maincrop
- Late maincrop

The early varieties grow much quicker but are lower yielding than maincrop potatoes. In most years they are also able to avoid blight (harvested before blight arrives). Maincrop potatoes produce a higher yield and can be stored over winter.

There are literally hundreds of varieties available.
They come in various shapes (round, oval, knobbly), sizes, colours (red, white, blue, purple and the flesh white, yellow, mottled or blue) and textures (waxy or floury). In Ireland the floury potatoes are much preferred.

Soil and site
Potatoes prefer an open, sunny and frost free site. The soil should be fertile and free-draining. Avoid low-lying frost pockets. They require a generous application of well-decomposed compost or manure. However, if too much fresh manure is incorporated in spring the potatoes often 'grow into leaf' at the expense of good tubers. This also makes them more susceptible to blight.

Planting
In Ireland, potatoes are traditionally planted in lazy beds.

Potatoes can either be planted in ridges (single row) or using a bed system (double row). If they are planted in ridges it is much easier to earth them up. Plant the seed tubers 10 to 15cm deep into fertile ground. Early potatoes can be chitted in order to get an earlier crop but in this case you may also get a setback from a late frost.

Chitting:
Buy your early seed potatoes in February and place them in shallow trays in a light frost free room. By mid March you will have strong, sturdy little green shoots.

Planting times:
First earlies: mid March (St. Patrick's Day)
Second earlies: early April
Maincrop: mid to late April

In Ireland, early potatoes were planted on St. Patrick's Day or on Good Friday. People believed the potatoes would be blessed and healthy.
Another belief was to plant the potatoes when a man can stand naked at the potato patch (for the non-Irish people this means he takes his top off!).

Spacing
Early potatoes:
Between plants: 25cm
Between rows: 50cm

Maincrop potatoes:
Between plants: 35cm
Between rows: 75cm

Rotation
Potatoes are susceptible to a wide range of diseases. Thus it is essential that they follow a strict rotation programme.

Plant care
In case there is a danger of frost and your potato shoots are just appearing you can protect them by earthing them up and covering the shoots with soil for protection.
When the haulm (shoot) is about 20cm high you should earth them up again. Use a draw hoe and pull loose soil against the haulm. Cover roughly half of the stem (10cm).

Harvesting and storing
Early potatoes can be harvested whenever you feel they are big enough. Some books recommend waiting until they form flowers but this is very dependent on the variety you grow. For example the variety 'Orla' does not flower at all in some years but they are still ready from July onwards. You can start digging one or two plants in late June to see how big they are. Never dig more than you need at a time as the tubers will not store well. The early crop should keep you going until October when you can harvest your maincrop.

Maincrop potatoes should be left in the ground until October even if you had to cut the stalks off for blight control much earlier. The reason for this is that the skins have to mature. This would happen naturally if the haulms are dying back.

If stored in boxes of sand in a cool, frost-free shed they will keep until April of the following year.

It is important that you harvest all potatoes, even the very smallest, otherwise they will become weeds for the following crop.

Potential problems

If you look in gardening books the list of potential potato troubles looks endless. The most common ones are:

- **Frost damage:**

Prevention: earth up shoots before a frosty spell or delay planting.

- **Blackleg:**

The symptoms include blackening of the stem at ground level and the leaves turn yellow and wilt. The disease is worse on heavy ground and during wet weather. There is no treatment for it. You should remove the diseased plants and burn them. The varieties Orla, Rooster and Charlotte are fairly resistant to blackleg.

- **Common scab:**

The symptoms are scaly patches on the potatoes. They are, however, only on the skin, so the eating quality is not affected. The varieties Nadine, Golden Wonder and King Edward have good resistance to scab.

- **Slugs:**

Slugs will move to your potatoes in late summer and eat little (or big!) holes into the tubers. It is important to keep your plot well weeded and the potatoes earthed up to minimise the problem. Varieties such as Sante, Charlotte, Nicola and Romano are more resistant to slugs than others.

- **Potato blight:**

See following page

How much to grow?

It is very difficult to guess how much land you need to grow all your potatoes. It depends how much you like them. In one garden we grew about 40m² and that provided more than enough potatoes for a family of four from July until April. One square metre may yield 5 to 7 kg of potatoes.

Varieties

There are literally hundreds of potato varieties available. In Ireland the favourite varieties are Kerr's Pink, Record and British Queens. Kerr's Pink is unfortunately very susceptible to potato blight and thus very difficult to grow organically. Epicure and Homeguard were traditionally grown as earlies. There are now many varieties available that have at least some tolerance to blight. However, most of them tend to be waxy rather than floury potatoes.

First earlies:
Sharpe's Express
Lady Christl (high yields of smooth skinned blight resistant potatoes with a waxy texture)
Homeguard
Pentland Javelin (smooth skinned, perfect for boiling)
Red Duke of York (medium sized oval tubers with an excellent flavour)
Colleen

Second earlies:
Catriona
Charlotte (one of my favourite varieties, excellent flavour, but maybe too waxy for the Irish taste)
Nadine
Orla
Roseval
Smile (red skin with prominent white eyes against the red skin looks like a smile)

Maincrop:
Arran Victory (blue skin, excellent flavour)
Cara (vigorous growth and good blight resistance)
Golden Wonder (apparently the best flavoured potato)
Nicola (yellow flesh, excellent flavour, salad potato)
Pink Fir Apple (definitely the best flavoured potato!)
Sante (excellent all purpose variety, long oval tubers with creamy flesh)
Sarpo Mira and Sarpo Aximo (Hungarian varieties with the best blight resistance)
Setanta (excellent blight resistance, high yield, Irish bred)

Heritage potatoes:
Champion (some people believe it's the best tasting potato of all with a floury texture and nutty flavour)
Shetland Black

Potato blight

For the first two centuries after its arrival, potatoes flourished throughout Europe and there are no historical records of potato blight (*Phytophthera infestans*) affecting the crop. The first incidence of blight was recorded in 1842 in Flanders in Belgium. Two years later in 1844 it first affected the crop in Ireland. The following years saw a series of disastrous crop failures which resulted in a widespread famine in Ireland.

What is potato blight?

Potato blight is a fungal disease which acts by attacking and killing the tissue of the leaves and tubers. The disease is spread by spores and it can destroy entire crops very quickly (within days in some cases). When a crop is affected by blight the first symptoms are small pale to dark green decaying spots on the leaves. Under certain conditions these grow rapidly into large, brown to black lesions often with a yellowish green margin outside the affected area. On young plants, blight travels quickly down the leaf stem and may infect the tubers. On more mature plants the disease progresses much more slowly. This means that an outbreak of blight early in the growing season has a much more severe effect on the crop.

When a potato is affected by blight, darkened areas appear on the skin and the flesh is discoloured by a reddish- brown rot. In addition to the disease travelling through the plant, tubers can become infected by blight through their eyes, wounds and directly through the skin. Potatoes affected by blight are inedible.

Factors affecting the incidence of blight

Susceptibility to blight is very dependent on a number of factors.

Temperature and relative humidity

Research has identified the conditions required for an outbreak of potato blight. These are named after the scientists who discovered them and when they occur a blight warning is issued by the authorities. A **Beaumont Period** occurs where there is a minimum temperature of 10° C and minimum relative humidity of 75% for 48 hours. A **Smith Period** occurs where there is a minimum temperature of 10° C for 48 hours and minimum relative humidity of 90% for at least 11 hours on each of two consecutive days.

Rainfall

Heavy rainfall greatly increases the incidence of tuber blight.

Rainwater is the most common way by which blight spores reach the soil to infect tubers. Heavy rainfall of at least 6mm over a short period is needed to wash blight spores down to the tubers and cause infection.

Potato variety

Some varieties of potato are much more resistant to infection than others. As the climatic conditions in Ireland especially in the West are ideal for the spread of blight - choosing a blight resistant variety is very important especially if you don't want to spray.

Controlling blight

Use of resistant varieties:

This is probably the single most effective way of dealing with the problem of potato blight. The most resistant varieties available at present are Setanta, Orla, Sarpo Axima, Sarpo Mira, Cara, Valor, which are well worth considering as they are very resistant to blight. However, the more blight resistant varieties tend to be less floury and therefore less appealing to the Irish palate.

Good agronomic practice:

- Tubers near the surface of drills are more frequently infected than those which are deeper. Planting in well formed drills will therefore provide protection to the developing tubers.
- Early planting of potatoes (ideally even chitted) will give them a good start. Their leaves will be more mature and thus more resistant when blight strikes.
- A good nutrient balance in the soil may lessen the incidence of blight. A high nitrogen content causes lush growth which is more susceptible to fungal diseases.
- Although rarely relevant in Ireland, irrigation increases the overall incidence of blight and should be avoided.
- When a certain amount of leaves (5%) are affected by blight, cutting off and removing the tops will minimise the risk of tuber infection. An interval of about 14 days between removal and lifting is recommended so that the skins can ripen before storage.

"It is easy to halve the potato where there is love"
Irish Saying

Pumpkin

Latin name:
Cucurbita maxima, pepo and
moschata
Family:
Cucurbitaceae
Related to:
Courgette, marrow, cucumber,
melon, squash.
Botanical classification:
The word pumpkin derives from
the Greek word *pepon* which means
'cooked by the sun'. The French
name for pumpkin 'potiron' means
'large mushroom'.

Introduction
Pumpkins are incredible
vegetables. They start off very
slowly, shiver with the slightest
wind but once they get going there
is nothing to stop them. You can
nearly watch them grow. They are
not well suited to a small garden as
they produce a mass of shoots and
leaves and may take over your
whole plot.

History
Pumpkins originated in Mexico
but are now grown all over the
world.

Soil and site
Pumpkins need a fertile, free-
draining soil that can hold plenty
of moisture. A generous
application of well-decomposed
compost is beneficial (about one
bucket per square metre).
They also need a sheltered place in
the garden as they really despise
strong winds.

Sowing
I usually sow seeds in early May
individually into 7cm pots. Ideally,
the pots are left in a propagator in
the greenhouse or on a south
facing windowsill. They may also
be fine in a tunnel without a
propagator, but plants have to be
covered up with fleece during cold
spells to protect them from frost
damage.

After about 3 weeks – or before the plants get pot bound – I pot them on into 12cm pots. The pots should be left in the greenhouse or indoors.

Planting

Start hardening off the plants at the end of May and plant out in early June. Do not plant if the weather forecast predicts cold windy spells which are quite common during this time.
The safest way would be to plant them under cloches which are covered with bionet.

Spacing

Please do not underestimate the space a pumpkin plant requires. The ideal planting distance is one plant every two metres. It is important to stick to this spacing but you can interplant some lettuce or annual spinach into the gaps at the early stages. They can be harvested before the pumpkins take over.

Rotation

Pumpkins belong to the cucurbit family. This family is not prone to any soil borne pests or diseases so there is no need to stick to a strict rotation. In fact they could be grown in the same place every year.

Plant care

From each pumpkin plant you will only get one large pumpkin (or two reasonably sized ones). In order to get one large fruit you should remove the smaller fruits and flowers so that all the energy of the plant goes into producing it.
Remember that pumpkins grow quite unruly. They will grow into pathways or over other vegetables so you need to keep them in place by moving the shoots back to where they should be.
Because of our wet summers and damp autumns I would recommend putting a slate or piece of timber underneath the ripening fruits to avoid rotting. Be aware though that the timber is also a slug trap so you need to check regularly what lies beneath otherwise you may create another problem!

Harvesting

Pumpkins should ideally be harvested when the leaves have died back. However it is not always possible to wait that long especially if there is a risk of frost. In that case pumpkins should be harvested before that. Cut carefully with the handle (fruit stalk) still attached to the pumpkin otherwise they will not store as well.
If they have not ripened enough you should move the fruits out into the sun during the day and move them back inside at night.

After a week of doing this they should be cured (ripe). Obviously if you want to eat them immediately there is no need to do that.

Storing
Pumpkins actually store for a surprisingly long time. If they have properly ripened they will store until March in a cool but frost free shed.

Potential problems
Apart from their sensitivity to cold and windy weather there are no specific pests or diseases that affect pumpkins. Slugs, however, like the newly planted pumpkins, so you need to protect them.

How much to grow?
Pumpkins are only suitable for large gardens. Everybody underestimates the space they require. Unless you have a large garden only one to two plants are sufficient. At least you'll have some fun at Halloween.

Varieties
Atlantic Giant (This pumpkin has the potential to reach 450kg)
Baby Bear (excellent pumpkin with small, uniform fruit)
Munchkin (small ribbed very attractive fruits)
Rouge Vif D'Etamp (large, heavily ribbed pumpkin with bright orange red skin)

"And forget not that the earth delights to feel your bare feet and the winds long to play with your hair"
-Kahlil Gibran

Radish

Latin name:
Raphanus sativus
Family:
Brassicaceae (also known as
Cruciferae)
Related to:
Cabbage, Brussels sprouts,
kohlrabi, cauliflower, radish,
turnip, swede.
Botanical classification:
Raphanus is a classical name
possibly from the Greek *ra*,
'quickly' and *phaino*, 'I appear', in
reference to the quick germination
of the seeds. *Sativus* means
cultivated.

Introduction
Radishes are a very fast growing,
crunchy small root vegetable. They
are excellent for a quick snack. Try
cutting them in half and eat with a
pinch of salt and butter. They are
really quite delicious.

History
Radishes originated in China and
were used in Egyptian, Greek and
Roman periods. Christopher
Columbus is credited with
introducing radishes to America.
Apparently the labourers who built
the pyramids were fed on radishes,
onions and garlic.

Types

Summer radish:
The more commonly known
radishes are the summer radishes.
There are many different shapes
and colours, round, cylindrical or
pointed; red, white or pink.

Winter radish:
Winter radishes are very rarely
grown in Ireland. My favourite
winter radish is the 'Black
Spanish Round', not because of its
taste but of memories of my grand-
mother Frida's recipe for chesty
colds. It really works wonders.

Recipe

Take a large Black Round Radish and cut it in half. Cut out a section of the radish and pierce a hole through the bottom with a knitting needle. Fill the hole with chrystallised brown sugar and place the radish over a glass. After a day or two the sugar starts to dissolve and a syrup flows into the glass. If you keep drinking this morning and evening the chesty cold will be gone within a couple of days.

Mooli Radish:

A more recent introduction are the oriental 'Mooli' radishes which can be grown like winter radishes.

Seed Pod Radish:

Some radishes are especially grown for their edible seed pods which are harvested when young and crisp. They really make a lovely addition to a salad bowl.

Leaf radish:

There are now varieties suitable for leaf production. Instead of harvesting the roots, the leaves are picked as a salad ingredient.

Soil and site

Radishes will grow in almost any reasonably fertile soil as long as the soil is moisture retentive. They will thrive in any open or sheltered site provided it is in full sun. The ideal pH ranges from 6 to 6.5.

Sowing

Summer radish

Radishes are one of the fastest vegetables to mature. You can harvest the roots from about 4 weeks after sowing. The only drawback is that once they are ready they will either become woody or go to seed. So you should only sow small quantities every now and then. Radishes are fairly hardy vegetables, so they can be sown from early April onwards (or even earlier in the warmer parts of the country) until late July.

I always sow seeds directly into the ground. They should be sown very thinly (about 2.5cm apart) in rows 15cm apart and about 1.5cm deep. Radish seeds are quite big so they can easily be spaced out accurately.

As soon as they have all germinated you can start thinning them.

For successional cropping you should sow small quantities every fortnight.

Winter radish

Winter radishes are somewhat easier. One sowing in July or August will produce radishes that can be stored over the winter in boxes of sand. Earlier sowings may run to seed.

Spacing

Summer radish
Row distance: 15cm
Distance in the row: 2-4 cm

Winter radish
Row distance: 25cm
Distance in the row: 20cm

Rotation

It is important to keep radishes in the brassica section of your rotation to prevent a build up of the numerous brassica pests and diseases. Don't be tempted to intercrop radishes with other vegetables.

Plant care

There is no maintenance required apart from thinning and keeping the plot weed free.

Harvesting

Summer radishes are ready four to six weeks after sowing. They have to be harvested straight away otherwise they will become woody and very hot flavoured.

Winter radishes are ready in October and can be stored in boxes of sand or in a plastic bag in the bottom of the fridge.

Potential problems:

The main pest of radishes is the fleabeetle. The symptoms are small 'shot-holes' through the leaves. A heavy infestation can destroy the crop. Covering the bed with bionet or fleece straight after sowing and during growth may prevent the attack.

They may also suffer from all the other brassica pests and diseases but the fact that they are harvested so quickly, these problems rarely occur.

How much to grow?

You will get about 100 radishes in one square metre. This shows that you should sow often and little.

Varieties

Summer radish:
Short Top Forcing (excellent and very reliable variety, very uniform)
Cherry Belle (scarlet globe and quick to mature)

Winter radish:
Black Spanish Round (dark black skin, white flesh, excellent storage capabilities)
China Rose (long roots with pink – red skin and white flesh)

Mooli radish:
April Cross F1 (long white roots that can be eaten raw)
Minowase (long white roots)

Seed pod radish:
Munchen Bier (grown for its tasty long seed pods with a succulent tangy taste)
Rats Tail (delicious seed pods on

large plants)
Leaf radish:
Saisai (grown for its delicious red veined leaves, ideal for salads)

*"What do I know of man's
destiny? I could tell you more about radishes"*
- Samuel Beckett

Scallion or spring onion

Latin name:
Allium cepa
Family:
Alliaceae (commonly known as
Alliums)
Related to:
Onion, shallot, garlic, leek, chives.
Botanical classification:
Allium is the Latin term for garlic;
now the name of all the onion fam-
ily, or from Celtic *all*, meaning
'pungent' or 'burning'. *Cepa* derives
from the Celtic *cep*, 'a head'.

Introduction
Scallions are a very popular salad
vegetable in Ireland. They are
grown for their small, white shanks
and tender, green stem and leaves.
They are very easy and quick to
grow but in order to get a
continuous supply you need to
make regular sowings.

Soil and site
Scallions require the same soil and
site condition as onions. The ideal
soil pH is 6.8 or above to get the
best crops.

Sowing
I usually grow them in modular
trays in a greenhouse or window

sill, ten seeds per cell and sow
them about 1.5cm deep. When
planting out the ten seedlings, do
not separate them, but plant them
together in a bunch. The
advantage of this is that you can
easily hoe between the bunches
and they are very easy to harvest
whole. They take about 4 weeks
from sowing to planting out.
Scallions do not last long once they
are ready in the garden. You should
thus sow small quantities at regular
intervals (every 2 to 3 weeks).

Sowing times

Scallions are fairly hardy crops, so they can be started off as early as late March in a greenhouse and the last sowing can be made in July.

Spacing

I plant bunches of ten seedlings together at a spacing of 25 x 30cm.

Rotation

It is absolutely essential to keep scallions in the allium section in your garden to minimise various soil-borne diseases such as white rot.

Plant care

Scallions prefer to grow on moist soil. If it is too dry they may develop a bulbous growth so watering may be necessary during dry spells.

Harvesting

Scallions are ready about 8 to 10 weeks after sowing. Harvesting is very easy if they are already growing in bunches. Simply pull out the bunches (or fork if your ground is too heavy), knock off some excess soil from the roots, cut off the tops so the bunches are about 25cm long and tie them together with a rubber band.

Always harvest the scallions as you need them as they will not keep well once they are harvested.

Potential problems

Scallions may suffer from the same pests and diseases as onions but to a much lesser extent because they mature much faster.

Downy mildew is the only problem I have encountered with scallions and only if I left the plants too long in the ground. There is a case for composting (or giving away) any excess scallions when they are over mature.

How much to grow?

If you require 2 bunches of scallions per week you can sow 6 bunches (10 seeds per module) every 3 weeks. At a spacing of 25cm x 30cm you will get 12 bunches per square metre.

Varieties

The most commonly sold variety in garden centres is White Lisbon. I am not a fan of it. It does not produce the scallions you know from the greengrocer. They are a lot smaller and spindlier.

There are two varieties which perform superbly in Ireland. These are:

Parade (excellent bunching onion with dark green leaves)

Ishikura Bunching

*"There is nothing pleasanter than spading
when the ground is soft and damp"*
- John Steinbeck

Scorzonera and Salsify

Latin name:
Szorzonera hispanica and Tragopogon porrifolius
Family: *Compositae* (also known as *Asteraceae*)
Related to:
Lettuce, chicory, Jerusalem artichokes, globe artichokes.
Botanical classification:
The name scorzonera probably derived from the French word *scorzon* which means serpent. The Spanish used the root for treating snake bites. Alternatively the name may derive from the Italian *scorza* meaning 'bark', and *nera* meaning 'black' which describes the root quite accurately.
The Latin name for salsify – *Tragopogon porrifolium* – derives from *tragos* meaning 'goat' and *pogon* meaning 'beard'. *Porrifolius* means 'leek-like leaves'.
The English name salsify derives from the Latin name *solsequium* indicating how the flowers follow the course of the sun.

Introduction

Most seed catalogues stock the seeds of salsify (also known as the Oyster Plant) and scorzonera and most gardening books describe how to grow them, but strangely

both of them are virtually unknown vegetables in Ireland. On the continent they are grown as delicacies for their delicious slender roots. Scorzonera especially is one of the tastiest vegetables I have ever tasted.
Scorzonera (black root) is a lot more reliable than salsify. Usually the roots grow straight, but they are so thin and long that they break when you try to dig them out.

History

Scorzonera was already known to the Greeks and Romans. It arrived in central Europe in the 16th century.

Soil and site

Both salsify and scorzonera prefer an open, sunny site with a deep, light soil with a pH of around 6.5.

Sowing

The seeds of salsify and scorzonera only last for one season so they should be bought new every year. The seeds should be sown directly into the ground (1cm deep) as transplanting them may cause forking of the roots. The best time to sow is in May. The seedlings should be thinned as soon as they have two true leaves.

Spacing

Between plants: 10cm
Between rows: 30cm

Rotation

Both scorzonera and salsify suffer from no specific pest or disease so you can use them anywhere in your garden.

Plant care

Apart from keeping the crop weed free there is little else to do. You may have to water the seedlings during dry spells.

Harvesting and storing

The roots are ready to harvest from October onwards. They can be left in the ground throughout the winter until they are required. Once they are harvested they should be used as soon as possible as they tend to shrivel quickly. Digging the roots seems to be a skill I have never managed to accomplish.

How much to grow?

Just try a few plants to see if you can grow them or if you like them.

Varieties

Salsify 'Sandwich Island'
Scorzonera 'Duplex'

*"People say that walking on water is a miracle;
But to me, walking peacefully on earth is the real miracle"*
- Thich Nhat Hanh

Shallot

Latin name:
Allium cepa Aggregatum Group
Family:
Alliaceae (commonly known as Alliums)
Related to:
Onion, scallion, garlic, leek, chives.
Botanical classification:
Allium is the Latin term for 'garlic'; now the name of all the onion family, or from Celtic *all*, meaning 'pungent' or 'burning'. *Cepa* derives from the Celtic *cep*, 'a head'.

Introduction

Shallots are a lot less popular than onions but some celebrity chefs try to change that fact. They are very easy to grow and have quite a distinctive flavour. They are also very interesting in the fact that if you plant one bulb (set) it multiplies and forms a clump of about eight bulbs.

Soil and site

Shallots require the same soil and site condition as onions. The ideal soil pH ranges from 6.5 to 7.

Planting

Shallots are best grown from sets (small shallots) which can be planted from the middle of March until the middle of April. Smaller sets are less likely to bolt than the larger ones. The sets should be planted so that the tip is still showing at the soil surface.

Spacing

Between plants: 25cm
Between rows: 30cm

Rotation

It is essential to keep shallots in the allium section in your garden to minimise various soil-borne diseases such as white rot.

Plant care

Apart from weeding there is little else to do. You have to be careful when you hoe so you do not damage the bulbs or disturb the roots. Hand weeding may be more appropriate at the later stages.

Harvesting

Shallots are ready a few weeks before onions. They are ready when three quarters of the leaves have fallen down and turned yellow. The best way to dry the bulbs is to leave them on the beds, ideally not touching each other, in full sun. Pull or fork out the shallots on a sunny day and leave them outside until the first rains. Then move them into an open shed and lay them on chicken wire or pallets in a single layer. You want to keep the rain off but still have good air circulation. You should also remove excess soil around the roots but do not remove the skins.

Storing

If you manage to dry the bulbs sufficiently they will store in a cool, ventilated shed until March.

Potential problems

Shallots suffer from the same pests and diseases as onions.

How much to grow?

If you eat 3 shallots per week which will store from mid August until mid March (28 weeks) you will need 82 shallots.

If you space the sets 25cm apart in the row and you fit 3 rows in a bed (bed width: 1.2m) and each set producing 8 shallots you will get 92 shallots per metre. In one metre you will get enough shallots from August until March.

Varieties

Unfortunately there is only a limited number of varieties available in garden centres.
If available try the following varieties:
Red Sun (deep red brown skin, very early, excellent flavour)
Golden Gourmet (yellow skin, firm even bulbs, stores well)

Spinach, Annual

Latin name:
Spinacia oleracea
Family:
Chenopodiaceae (Goosefoot Family)
Related to:
Perpetual spinach, chard, beetroot, sugar beet.
Botanical classification:
Spinacia derives from the Latin *spina*, 'a prickle', in allusion to the prickly seeds. *Oleracea* means 'cultivated'.

Introduction
Spinach is an annual plant that produces a quick crop especially if the weather is cool and damp. In hot weather the plant tends to bolt prematurely. Thus it is an excellent vegetable for spring and autumn.

History
Spinach may have originated in southwest Asia or the western Himalayas. It was first cultivated by the Persians as a medicinal plant, then spread to China in the 7th century and into Europe in the 11th century. It only reached England and Ireland in the 16th century.

Soil and site
Spinach loves a rich, fertile soil with a high nitrogen content. The preferred pH value is between 6.5 and 7.5. It will benefit from generous compost or composted manure applications.

Sowing and planting
Spinach can easily be sown directly in your garden or, if preferred raised in modular trays inside (windowsill or polytunnel).
 The recommended sowing depth is 1.5cm. I generally sow 4 seeds in each modular cell.
As annual spinach has a short life in the garden you may consider doing successional sowings (every three weeks) from early April until

August. In a mild, sheltered garden you could try and sow a winter variety in August and September. The summer sowings should be in part shade to reduce the risk of bolting.

Spacing

Plant spacing: 7cm for baby-leaf spinach and 15cm for normal sized spinach.
Row spacing: 25cm

It is important to thin the seedlings early to the recommended spacing as this discourages bolting.

Rotation

Spinach and other members of the *Chenopodiaceae* family are not prone to any specific pests and diseases so you do not have to be too fussy about rotation. You could use them as 'flexi-crops' or gap fillers.

Annual spinach is an excellent vegetable for intercropping. It is a neutral vegetable (not susceptible to any specific disease) and not related to the troublesome families such as the brassicas or alliums. Due to its short-lived nature and low growth habit, it can be used anywhere in your vegetable garden to quickly fill a space.

Intercropping options:
- Spring sowing before brassicas are planted in late May.
- Between widely spaced crops until they need the space.
- Mixed cropping with any vegetable.

Plant care

Never let the soil dry out. Water regularly during dry spells and keep the plot weed free at all times.

Harvesting

You can harvest spinach at the baby leaf stage about 40 days after sowing and ordinary spinach is ready after about 50 days from sowing. Harvest fresh leaves as required by twisting or cutting the outside leaves of the plant (as low as possible).
It can also be used as a cut-and-come again crop. You simply cut the entire plant at about 5cm above ground level and after two to three weeks you can do the same again. I would only use this technique with spinach if I am in a rush as the yield is reduced. Young spinach leaves make an excellent addition to a salad.

Potential problems

Slugs and aphids are the main pests. Downy mildew is the most common disease. The symptoms are white fluffy patches on the underside of the leaves. If most of the leaves are diseased it is better to remove the plants and start again. Some varieties are more resistant to the disease.
The main problem with annual spinach, however is bolting.

An old gardening book describes spinach as holding the world's record for bolting.

A combination of the following recommendations may slow it down:
- Prepare and feed soil properly.
- Sow summer crops in part shade.
- Thin plants early.
- In summer sow seeds direct into the ground rather than in modules.
- Keep the bed moist at all times during dry spells.
- Grow bolt resistant varieties.

How much to grow?

If you love spinach grow one square meter every 3 weeks.

Varieties

Emilia F1 (dark green hybrid for summer cropping , bolt resistant)
Galaxi F1 (very hardy variety, suitable for autumn, winter and spring cropping
Palco F1 (quick to establish and relatively slow to bolt, excellent resistance to mildew)
Tornado F1 (excellent for growing in the summer, good bolting tolerance and mildew resistance)

"Come forth into the light of things, let nature be your teacher"
- William Wordsworth

Spinach, Perpetual

Latin name:
Beta vulgaris subsp. *flavescens*
Family:
Chenopodiaceae (Goosefoot Family)
Related to:
Swiss chard, beetroot, annual spinach, sugar beet.
Botanical classification:
Beta is the Latin word for beetroot. *Vulgaris* means 'common'.

Introduction

It is also known as spinach beet and leaf beet. It is from the same family as beetroot, but it is grown for its large green leaves. It is one of the few vegetables which has never been taken up by plant breeders. There are very few named varieties of perpetual spinach around, the most commonly sold by far is called perpetual spinach. It is a lot easier to grow compared to annual spinach. It gives much higher yields, is less likely to bolt and it lasts much longer. However, the annual spinach has a better flavour and is a lot more tender.

Soil and site

Perpetual spinach will do well in any fertile soil. It is a greedy plant: the more compost or composted manure you give it, the higher it will yield.

Sowing and planting

Perpetual spinach is very easy to establish. It can either be sown directly into the garden or first raised in modular trays in a greenhouse. If you sow it directly into the ground you sow individual seeds 2.5cm deep in drills.

If you raise it in modular trays sow one seed per cell. You will notice that from the one seed about 3-5 seedlings appear. They are like beetroot – clusters of seeds. In order to get a good strong plant you need to thin out the seedlings to leave just the strongest one in each cell.

The same applies to the direct sown crop.

Two sowing dates are sufficient to get a continuous supply of perpetual spinach:

- Mid April and early June

Spacing

Between plants: 30cm
Between rows: 30cm

Rotation

Perpetual spinach is not susceptible to any specific pests and diseases, so you don't have to rotate it.

Plant care

It's really such an easy vegetable to grow. All you need to do is to keep the crop weed free and well watered during dry spells. It's also beneficial to remove the lower leaves which turn brown if not harvested on time.

Harvesting

Harvest the leaves continually throughout the growing season by twisting them away from the base of the plant. It is a down, push, twist movement. Try it a few times to get practice. It is much better for the plant than cutting it and ending up with diseased little stumps.

How much to grow?

Five plants sown in mid April and five in June will give you spinach from June until October.
This will take up less than one square metre for each sowing.

Varieties

Perpetual spinach (the most common variety)
Erbette (light green, crinkly leaves)
Note:
Plant breeders have shown very little interest in this vegetable. This reflects the absence of varieties. The one variety which is most available is simply called Perpetual spinach, like the vegetable itself.

"If one really loves nature, one can find beauty everywhere"

- Vincent Van Gogh

Squash

Latin name:
Cucurbita maxima, pepo and
moschata
Family:
Cucurbitaceae
Related to:
Courgette, marrow, cucumber,
melon.

Introduction:

Squashes are one of the most vigorous vegetables. Some varieties can easily cover an area of 5 square metres, rambling over any neighbouring crop. Thus they are not well suited to a small garden. You can, however, experiment growing them in more unusual places – on top of an old compost heap, or up trellises.

There are two types of squashes:

- Summer squashes
- Winter squashes

For both types there are bush and trailing varieties. The bush plants are a lot better behaved and require a lot less space than the trailing varieties but the yield is lower.

Summer squashes are grown and harvested like courgettes. There are only a few varieties available but some of them are excellent.

Winter squashes are grown for storage. The fruit is harvested in October before the first frost and stored. There is a huge choice of varieties available. Immature fruits of winter squash can also be used throughout the season.

History

The name 'Squash' is an abbreviation of the native American word *askutashash* which means 'eaten raw or uncooked'.

Soil and site

Squashes need a very fertile, free-draining soil which can hold plenty of moisture. A generous application of well-decomposed compost is beneficial (about one bucket per square metre).

They also need a sheltered place in the garden as they really despise strong wind.

Sowing

Squashes are very tender plants.

I usually sow seeds in early May individually into 7cm pots. Ideally the pots are left in a propagator in the greenhouse or on the windowsill at home (south facing). They may also be fine in a tunnel without a propagator but plants have to be covered up with fleece during cold spells to protect them from frost damage.

After about 3 weeks – or before the plants get pot bound – I pot them on into 12cm pots which are still left in the greenhouse or indoors.

Planting

Start hardening the plants off towards the end of May and plant out in early June. Do not plant if the weather forecast predicts cold windy spells which are quite common during this time. The safest way would be to plant them under cloches which are covered with bionet.

Spacing

Bush varieties: 1.2m apart each way.
Trailing varieties: 2m apart each way.

Rotation

Squashes belong to the cucurbit family. This family is not prone to any soil-borne pests or diseases so you do not need to be too fussy with rotation.

Plant care

Keep the plants weed free, especially in the early stages as it will be very difficult later on to get to the weeds. If they are well weeded at the start the large leaves will prevent new weeds from germinating.

As with pumpkins, squashes may try to grow over neighbouring vegetables, so they need to be kept in check, either by shortening some shoots or by moving them back to their allocated space.

Hand pollination:

In cold, wet weather (when few insects are around) you can pollinate the flowers by hand. This will increase your chances to get fruits.

Squash plants have separate male and female flowers. They are easily distinguishable by looking at the flower stalk. The male stalk is plain and the female flower carries a small fruit on its stalk.

You transfer the pollen from the male to the female flowers with a soft brush or remove the male flower and rub it onto the open blooms of the female flowers.

Harvesting and storing

Summer squashes should be harvested every week. Some varieties such as Sunburst F1 are very prolific. If you let the fruit mature the yield will be reduced.

Winter squashes are harvested in late autumn before the first frost. If you want to store squashes, leave the fruits to mature on the vine at least until October. The mature fruits have hard outer shells. Use a sharp knife to cut the stems (or handles) of the fruits to be stored and leave the stem attached to the fruit. If the leaves of the plants are still green that means that the fruit is not yet cured and will not store for long. You should then leave the fruits out in a sunny spot for about ten days and only move them in if frost threatens. They will then store in a dry, fairly cool location until March.

Potential problems

Squash plants need to be protected from slugs at the early stages straight after planting out. Like all other cucurbits they are very sensitive to cold and windy weather. It is highly beneficial to plant them under a cloche covered with bionet for the first month. During unfavourable weather they may fail to set fruit. You may have to do some 'artificial insemination' (see courgette section).

How much to grow?

Two to three plants are sufficient otherwise you will have no room left for anything else. Squashes, however are exciting plants to grow and the fact that there are so many different varieties around, makes it very difficult to restrict yourself to just a few plants.

Varieties
Summer squash:
Patty Pan (pale green scalloped-edged fruits, needs to be harvested regularly)
Sunburst F1 (highly attractive and delicious bright yellow flat scalloped-edged fruits, very high yielding)

Winter squash:
Butternut F1 (the best known and one of the most delicious squashes but needs a good summer to do well in Ireland, trailing habit)
Crown Prince F1 (one of the best flavoured squashes, steel grey skin and orange flesh, store well, trailing habit)
Delicata –Cornell Strain (my favourite one for taste, also known as the sweet potato squash, cream colour with green stripes, needs a good summer to do well, bush habit)
Sweet Dumpling (produces a large number of small fruits with striped skin and creamy white flesh, bush habit)
Table Ace F1 (dark green acorn shaped fruits weighing up to 1 kg with a nutty flavour, trailing habit)
Turk's Turban (turban shaped, highly decorative and edible fruit, very prolific and well suited to Irish conditions, trailing habit)

Uchiki Kuri (orange/red pear-shaped fruit, nutty flavour, suited to Irish conditions)
Vegetable Spaghetti (the fruit can be baked whole and the flesh can be scooped out - it looks like spaghetti)

"Winter squashes are the forgotten vegetables. Almost no vegetable is as easy to grow or keep. With fertile soil, full sun and ample water, vines take off. And after plants become established, they're so carefree, it's easy to forget them until fall when their rediscovery makes the harvest that much sweeter"
- Andy Tomolonis

Swede

Latin name:
Brassica napus Napobrassica Group
Family:
Brassicaceae (also known as
Cruciferae)
Related to:
Cabbage, Brussesls sprouts, kale,
cauliflower, radish, turnip, kohlrabi
Botanical classification:
Brassica derives from the Celtic
bresic, the name for cabbage.

Introduction
Swedes are very closely related to
turnips. The name swede is an
abbreviation of Swedish turnip.
Swedes generally have yellow flesh
as opposed to the white flesh of
turnips.
Swedes are an ideal vegetable for
Irish conditions. They prefer the
mild and moist conditions and they
are also one of the highest yielding
vegetables.

History
It is believed that swedes evolved
as a cross of cabbage with turnip,
followed by a spontaneous
chromosome doubling. This
evolution occurred in relatively
recent history, probably in Sweden.

Soil and site
Swedes will grow in a range of
soils provided they are reasonably
fertile. Compost application is
highly beneficial. The ideal pH
ranges from 6 to 6.8.

Sowing and planting
In theory, swedes can be sown
directly outdoors in drills but you
will get much better results if you
raise them in modular trays. You
sow one seed in each cell 2cm
deep and keep the modular tray in
a tunnel or on the windowsill. The
seeds will germinate within a week
and after about 4 weeks they are
ready to be hardened off and can

then be planted out.

From two sowings you can harvest swedes for many months of the year:

First sowing: mid April

Second sowing: late May

Spacing

Large swedes:

Between plants: 30cm

Between rows: 30cm

Small swedes:

Between plants: 20cm

Between rows: 30cm

Rotation

It is absolutely essential to keep swedes in the brassica section of your rotation to prevent a build up of the numerous brassica pests and diseases.

Plant care

Keep the soil hoed and watered during dry periods. This will prevent the roots from getting tough and woody. You should also check regularly for any signs of pest damage, especially cabbage white butterfly caterpillars.

Harvesting and storage

From the April sowing, the swedes can be harvested as required at whichever size you prefer from around August onwards. The crop which was sown in June is best left in the ground until late October. Then you can either store the roots

in boxes of sand or you can risk leaving them in the ground. They can easily withstand some frost but I suggest that if your ground becomes waterlogged in winter you had better store them safely.

Potential problems

Swedes are susceptible to all the brassica troubles particularly the fleabeetle which can decimate young seed leaves. To minimise this danger you can raise the seedling in modular trays so they are already more established when planted out.

Apart from the fleabeetle, swedes grow much healthier than the other brassicas.

How much to grow?

Winter swedes:

If you eat 1 reasonable sized swede per week, storing from October until the end of April (28 weeks) you will need 28 swedes. If you space the seeds 25cm in the row and you fit 4 rows in a bed (bed width: 1.2m) you will get 16 swedes per metre.

In 2 metres you will get enough carrots from October to April.

Summer swedes:

With the early sowing you can plant one meter of a bed to give you 1 swede every week for 12 weeks (from August until the end of October).

Varieties:
Acme Purple Top (what a terrible name for this excellent variety)
Helenor (good quality globe shaped roots, sweet taste)
Gowrie (purple skinned variety with excellent disease resistance)
Marian (a purple top variety with some resistance to clubroot and mildew)
Ruby (a purple top variety, excellent flavour)

*"No occupation is so delightful to me as the culture of the earth,
no culture comparable to that of the garden....
But though an old man, I am but a young gardener"*
- Thomas Jefferson

Sweetcorn

Latin name:
Zea mays
Family:
Gramineae
Related to:
All grasses
Botanical classification:
Zea derives from the Greek.

Introduction

There are many downsides to growing sweetcorn in Ireland, but the one upside is the incredible taste of a freshly harvested and cooked sweetcorn. There is absolutely no comparison to a shop bought one. The reason for this is that once the cob has been harvested the sugar is steadily converted into starch.

The trouble really is that this vegetable needs a lot more sun and warmth than we usually have in Ireland. It is also very low yielding, producing only two cobs per plant.

History

Sweetcorn was first cultivated in Mexico around 7000 BC. It became a staple crop in North America from 800 AD onwards. It was only introduced to Europe after the 16th century.

Soil and site

Sweetcorn requires a fertile, free draining, but moisture retentive soil. A generous application of well-rotted compost is essential. Only grow sweetcorn if your garden is in full sun, sheltered from cold winds and ideally south facing. If you don't have these site conditions you may have to buy yourself a greenhouse!

Sowing

To prolong the growing season you should start sweetcorn off indoors, ideally on a heating bench at 20°C. Alternatively a south-facing windowsill will do. You can sow individual seeds in small pots (7cm) 2.5cm deep in early May. The plants need to be hardened off before planting out.

Planting

Sweetcorn should not be planted out before the beginning of June when the soil has warmed up sufficiently. The use of a cloche at the early stages would be highly beneficial if not even necessary. I would cover the cloche with bionet rather than plastic.

Spacing

Between plants: 45cm
Between rows: 45cm

Sweetcorn should be planted in rectangular blocks as opposed to single lines. This will ensure successful wind pollination.
The male flowers are on top of the plant and the female flowers are the tassels at the end of the cobs. Each little silky strand has to receive a pollen grain to develop a kernel. You may have noticed some kernels missing from a cob. They didn't get pollinated.

Rotation

Sweetcorn is the only vegetable in the Graminae family and there is no risk of any soil-borne pest or disease affecting it. So really you can plant it wherever it suits you.

Plant care

If you have protected your plants with cloches you have to check them regularly and remove them before the plants reach the top. Keep the crop weed free especially in the early stages but be careful when hoeing so as not to disturb the roots. It would be beneficial to add a shovelful of a good compost soil mix at the base of each plant.

Harvesting

In late summer you should check regularly to see if the tassels at the end of the cobs wither and turn brown. When this happens double check if the cob is ripe by carefully peeling off part of the sheath. You then squeeze a kernel and if a milky juice comes out it's ready to harvest. If it is clear liquid you have to wait a bit longer.

Potential problems

Apart from the lack of sun and warmth there is nothing that bothers sweetcorn.

Varieties

There has been a lot of plant breeding for sweetcorn. You get the traditional varieties and super sweet types which contain up to twice as much sugar.

Traditional varieties:

Black Aztec (seeds are blue black, can be eaten fresh or dried)
Golden Bantam (very good quality, sweet flavour)

Supersweet varieties:

Earligold F1 (an early vigorous variety, good choice for difficult areas)

Sweet Nugget F1 (excellent yield of long, uniform cobs)

Swift F1 (one of the best flavoured sweetcorn, exceptionally sweet and succulent kernels)

"....pray what more can a reasonable man desire, in peaceful times, in ordinary noons, than a sufficient number of ears of sweet-corn boiled, with the addition of salt?"
- Henry David Thoreau

Swiss Chard

Latin name:
Beta vulgaris subsp. *cicla*
Family:
Chenopodiaceae (Goosefoot Family)
Related to:
Spinach, beetroot, sugar beet.
Botanical classification:
Beta is the Latin word for beetroot.
Vulgaris means 'common'. *Cicla* is the old Sicilian name for Silver beet or Swiss Chard.

Introduction
It is also known as silver chard, silver beet and seakale beet. It is from the same family as beetroot but it is grown for its dark green leaves and broad white stalks which can be used like spinach. The Italians only use the stalks and discard the leaves. In other countries they do the opposite. But you can use everything. There are other types: Ruby Chard with red stems and red-veined leaves, Rainbow Chard with multi-coloured stems and leaves and also recently introduced a Yellow Chard with yellow stems and veins. They are all very decorative crops suitable for flower borders.

History
It can be traced back to the ancient Greek times. The Romans introduced it to central and northern Europe and from there to China and Persia. The wild form can be found all around the Mediterranean and British coasts.

Soil and site
Chard will do well in any fertile soil provided that plenty of compost or composted manure has been applied (1 bucket per sqm). The ideal soil pH is 6.5 – 7.5. If the soil is acidic, ground limestone should be applied. Chard is not even too fussy about the site. I've grown it successfully in fairly exposed places.

Sowing and planting

Chard can be raised exactly the same way as perpetual spinach (see p.133).

Spacing

Between plants: 30cm
Between rows: 30cm

Rotation

Chard is not susceptible to any specific pests or diseases, so there is no need to follow a strict rotation.

Plant care

Keep the crop weed free and watered during dry spells. It is also beneficial to remove the lower leaves which turn brown if not harvested on time.

Harvesting

Just like perpetual spinach, harvest the leaves on a regular basis by twisting them away from the base of the plant.

How much to grow?

Five plants sown in mid April and five in June will give you spinach from June until November.
This will take up less than one square metre from each sowing.

Varieties

Swiss Chard (long, thick white stems and dark green leaves)
Rhubarb Chard (red stemmed version of Swiss chard)
Rainbow Chard (mixture of various coloured stems and leaves, very ornamental)

"When the sun rises, I go to work
When the sun goes down I take my rest,
I dig the well from which I drink,
I farm the soil which yields my food,
I share creation,
Kings can do no more"
-Chinese Proverb

146

Turnip

Latin name:
Brassica napus Rapifera Group
Family:
Brassicaceae (also known as
Cruciferae)
Related to:
Cabbage, Brussesls sprouts, kale,
cauliflower, radish, turnip,
kohlrabi.
Botanical classification:
Brassica derives from the Celtic
bresic, the name for cabbage.

Introduction
What is commonly known in
Ireland as a turnip is really a swede
so if you want to grow your
turnips do buy a packet of swede
seeds and refer to the swede
chapter for the relevant
information. The 'real' turnips are
less used or grown in Ireland.
However, they are very easy to
grow and are very quick to mature.
You can often harvest them 8 to
10 weeks after sowing. Their roots
may be flat, round or elongated;
the flesh is white or yellow.

History
The cultivated turnip originates
from the Nile and Indus region
and has been a favourite since
Roman times.

Legend and Lore
Turnips were considered to be an
aphrodisiac. "It augmenteth the
seed of man and provoketh carnal
lust" - Sir Thomas Elliot 1539

Soil and site
Turnips prefer cool, moist
conditions. They will grow in a
range of soils provided they are
reasonably fertile. Compost
application is highly beneficial.
The ideal pH is 6.8. If your soil is
more acidic you should add ground
limestone.

Sowing and planting
Outdoors from early April
onwards (if soil conditions allow).
They should be sown thinly in
shallow drills 2cm deep. The
seedlings should be thinned to the
recommended spacing as soon as
possible to prevent the roots from
intertwining with each other. In

order to get a continuous supply of turnips, you can sow from April until July every three weeks.

Spacing
Between plants: 15cm (or 10cm if you want to harvest the thinnings)
Between rows: 25cm

Rotation
It is absolutely essential to keep turnips in the brassica section of your rotation to prevent a build up of the numerous brassica pests and diseases.

Plant care
Keep well weeded and water during dry spells.

Harvesting and storage
Baby turnips can be harvested when the roots are about 5cm in diameter. Instead of the recommended 15cm spacing between plants you could space them 10cm apart and harvest every second root while it is still small. Turnips should always be eaten fresh. They are not as well suited for long term storage as swedes.
From the successional sowings you can expect to harvest turnips from June until October.

Potential problems
Turnips are susceptible to all the brassica troubles and, as with the swede, fleabeetles cause most havoc.

How much to grow?
Sow a few plants every three weeks.

Varieties
Market Express F1 (pure white early Japanese type, cold tolerant)
Milan Purple Top (very reliable variety with purple tops and a white base)
Oasis (very unusual melon flavoured variety)
Snowball (small quick growing variety with white skin)
White Globe (smooth round roots of white flesh with bright purple tops)

"This diamond has so many carats it's almost a turnip"
- Richard Burton

Jerusalem Artichokes: Fuseau (white), Gerard (red)

Red Cabbage Variety: Rodynda

Dwarf French Bean Variety: Purple Teepee

Borage an edible flower which lifts the spirits

Thien watering in the glass house

Country Vegetable Garden, Beltra, Co Sligo

Probably the best beetroot variety: Pablo

My favourite pea variety: Greenshaft

A mixture of lettuce varieties

Oca – a crop for the future

Worms – our best friends in the garden

Springtime at home in Milkwood

Example of intercropping (lettuce with Redbor kale)

Yellow round courgette with edible flowers

Thien digging the soil

Isabella and Anna-Maya shelling peas for dinner

Joanna admiring the seaweed at mermaids cove

Willis' walled garden in Beltra

Comfrey - used as a liquid feed

Swede (known as a turnip in Ireland)

Globe Artichoke

Dutch Cabbage

Butterhead Lettuce ~Dynamite, resistant to aphids

Anna-Maya sampling the apples

Isabella tying up the vines

In the garden at home

Planning the Vegetable Garden

It is impossible to prescribe set plans for gardens as every garden has its unique character. Even established gardens still change and evolve.

Decide on the size

You will be surprised how much produce you will get out of a small plot of land. People often think that you will need at least an acre to feed a family of four. In fact, an area of 200m² (i.e. 20m x 10m) will be enough to produce all the vegetable needs while in season.

Note: One acre of land can feed 20 families with vegetables. One acre can't even feed a cow. If we run out of food we may have to become vegetarian. If you only want to grow a wide range of fresh vegetables and herbs and buy in your potatoes, 80sqm is sufficient.

For new gardeners the best advice is to start small. It is very discouraging to plant more than you can look after and then the pleasure may turn into a chore. In a garden as small as 10m² you can get all your greens (salads, spinach, scallions, courgette).

The size you choose depends entirely on you, on your skills, fitness, motivation, the size of your garden and your knowledge of vegetable growing. I would strongly recommend not to take on too much in the first year, but plan your plot in such a way that you can extend it in the future.

Even if you don't have a garden you can grow salads and many vegetables in hanging baskets, windowboxes and other suitable containers.

How much time do I need to grow my own vegetables?

It is true that growing your own vegetables takes more time compared with growing ornamental shrubs and trees. This is especially true in spring when you are busy with soil preparation, sowing, planting and caring for your crops until they fill out the beds and weed growth slows down. In summer there is much less to do apart from the occasional weeding and hoeing. Harvesting your own vegetables is one of the most satisfying aspects of gardening.

Between 4 to 8 hours per week is sufficient during the busy spring season to care for a vegetable plot which could feed a family of four. After that there will be substantially less work. If you do the right job at the right time and do it properly you can save yourself hours of unnecessary work.

Buy a diary

A garden diary is one of the best tools for a vegetable gardener. You should keep a record of what you grew and where. It is also very helpful to list the vegetable varieties and sowing dates. If you find that you struggle with a particular vegetable the first thing to check is if your soil is fertile enough. If the soil is healthy you should consider changing the variety. There are big differences between individual vegetable varieties and some may be a lot more suited to your conditions than others. The next thing to consider is the sowing date. Problems usually occur if you sow too early.

With the help of your diary you will be able to create your own per-fect recipe with the most suitable varieties and sowing dates for your own garden.

Decide what you want to grow

If you are new to vegetable gardening you may consider starting off with some of the easily grown vegetables such as potatoes, cabbage, swede, perpetual spinach, lettuce, radish, courgette, etc.

Think about what you really want to eat before you plan your garden. So many gardeners, and I'm one of the worst culprits, grow vegetables which they know will never be eaten. They just love growing them.

Don't grow more than you need. Hopefully the information in the vegetable section will give you an idea as to how much space you need to give to each vegetable.

Common mistakes we all make

Sowing and planting too early in the year:

This is probably the most common mistake everyone makes. Remember those lovely sunny warm days in March or April when we get that urge to go out into the garden and sow a few seeds. The instructions on seed packets and information from UK books aren't helping either. Irish conditions are a lot different due to the wind and rain and often heavy soils, so the ground won't warm up as quickly in the spring as it does in England. If you were to sow your parsnips in March like everyone recommends you may have only a 30% success rate. If sown in April it will increase to 60% so why not sow them in May when you are more or less guaranteed a perfect crop. So, don't be fooled by those misleading wonderful spring days. They are always followed by a cold spell. For most vegetables, May is by far the best month for sowing or planting out.

There are a few exceptions. The following list includes vegetables that can or should be sown or planted outdoors before May:

Broad beans (October or March/April)
Garlic (October or March)
Onions (March/April)
Peas (April)
Potatoes (March/April)
Shallots (March/April)

Most other vegetables can be raised in modular trays in April and planted out in May or sown directly outdoors in May.

Wrong choice of plants:

Warmth loving plants such as cucumbers, tomatoes, peppers, aubergines, climbing French beans and sweetcorn will always do poorly if grown outside, especially in northern or exposed areas. My advice is to grow them in a poly-tunnel and concentrate on plants which are suitable to your area. Alternatively, create a suitable micro-climate for these crops by growing them next to a warm sheltered south-facing wall.

Plants are spaced too close together:

When we sow seeds directly into the ground we always sow more seeds than are necessary for that space. When the seedlings start to appear we must ensure that they are spaced correctly so that they can develop fully.

We have to **thin out** seedlings to the recommended spacing. This involves pulling out all surplus seedlings leaving only the strong ones at the correct stations. If this is not done the vegetables will never develop fully and may look more stunted and thus become more susceptible to diseases. I have seen situations where 50 seedlings have to be thinned to leave just one.

Problems with plant raising:

There could be various reasons for seeds failing to germinate:

- Seeds were sown too early when the soil was too cold.
- Seed compost could have dried out.
- Seeds were not viable anymore

(too old or poor storage).
- Seeds could be eaten be mice (especially peas and beans).
- Seedlings could be eaten by slugs.

Leggy seedlings:
After germination seedlings become thin and leggy. The reason is they didn't get enough light which is commonly the case early in the year. Even on a south facing windowsill or a greenhouse there is insufficient natural light until the end of February. So either delay sowings until the end of February or get artificial lamps to supplement the natural light.

Choosing the best site for your vegetable plot

One of the most important aspects of gardening is a proper assessment of the site and the soil of the garden.
When deciding where to plant your vegetable garden, choose the best available location by keeping the following factors in mind.

a) History
It is well worth finding out the history of your garden or plot. You may be lucky enough if there was a vegetable garden there in the past as this will most definitely be the most suitable spot again for you. People have improved little plots of land for vegetable growing with generous applications of manure. If there is nobody who remembers you will have to some detective work.

Simply take a spade and dig a few small sample holes around your garden. Hopefully you will notice some differences in the soil. What you are looking for is the patch where the spade slides into the soil quite easily, where the soil is a lot darker and deeper than the surrounding soil and where the soil crumbles a lot easier when rubbed between your fingers. If you are lucky enough to find this patch you are already halfway there to grow excellent vegetables. If you can't find it is not the end of the world either but you have to work a bit harder and work in fairly large quantities of good quality mature compost.

If you take over an existing vegetable plot, the soil is likely to be good, but you may also encounter more weeds, pests and diseases.

b) Easy access for you
It is of great advantage to site your vegetable plot as close as possible to your kitchen for your own convenience. You can keep a close eye on how your seeds and plants are doing and also harvesting the crops is much easier. You should also consider where you will keep tools and other supplies.

c) Aspect (south facing gardens are warmer)

A south-facing garden is ideal for vegetable growing, because there is more light and the soil warms up faster in spring. This allows you to sow and plant out vegetables earlier. You may also be able to grow slightly more tender vegetables. If your garden isn't south facing you may have to delay sowing and planting of your crops.

d) Light and shade

A place in the sun is without doubt the main precondition for the siting of your vegetable plot. The more sun hours your vegetable plot gets the higher the yield and the better the taste of your vegetables will be. This is extremely important in Ireland with lower light intensities. There is no such thing as too much light in Ireland.

e) Wind and shelter

Protection from strong wind is essential. Wind slows down plant growth as it lowers the temperature and increases the evaporation of the plants. It has been shown that a sheltered garden can be up to 3°C higher than an adjacent non-sheltered one. Strong winds may also knock over tall plants such as Brussels sprouts or broad beans, damage pea and runner bean supports or blow away cloches. On the other hand if your garden is too

sheltered, fungal diseases such as grey mould or potato blight or pests such as aphids may spread faster.

Winds dry out soils which in wet areas can be an advantage.
A hedge across the main wind direction of the garden will provide shelter. Hedges are by far the best windbreaks. Hedges look attractive and let the wind filter through. They also provide food and shelter for birds and insects, especially if native species are chosen.

In very exposed areas a newly planted hedge may need the initial support of an artificial windbreak. For every 1m of height of a good windbreak you will get 10m of protection on the leeward side. In a large garden you may need a second smaller shelterbelt.

f) Frost pockets

Cold air sinks down and flows downwards. A frost pocket is created if the cold air flow is blocked through walls or thick hedges. In general any area where frost lingers (usually low lying areas) should be avoided.

Competition from tree roots

You really cannot get away with planting your vegetables under trees or even close to trees. There is this misconception that the tree roots extend to where the tree crown ends. This is completely untrue! Tree roots spread much further than that, roughly about the same distance as the height of the tree.

Gradient / Slope

A slope of 1-2% ideally south-facing is the best as this will help with drainage. Any more and there is the danger of topsoil being washed away by heavy rain. On steeper slopes, terracing your garden (with retaining walls) would be an alternative.

Access to water

An accessible water supply is essential for protected cropping and for plant raising. In dry areas or on sandy soil it may be necessary to water outdoors especially after transplanting. Rainwater is better than tap water.

Climate

The micro-climate in a garden can be influenced by using shelterbelts or planting next to south-facing walls. The overall climate however can't be changed. There is a big difference if you want to grow vegetables in Cork, Dublin or Leitrim. There is a much better chance to grow warmth loving and early vegetables in the warmer parts of the country.

Electricity

A power supply is only important if you consider raising your plants on a heating bench in a small greenhouse. The greenhouse is best sited close to the house so you can check and care for your seedlings regularly. In this case you could bring out a waterproof extension from the house.

Relationship between garden and surroundings

Your garden can be designed to screen ugly buildings or enhance attractive local features by borrowing focal points. For example a church steeple or mountain top can be incorporated into your design.

Protection from animals

And finally you really have to consider protecting your plot from the larger animals. Rabbits and hares like your carrots and cabbages just as much as you do.

Soil

With gardening, everything starts with the soil. To me there is no such thing as a green fingered gardener – only brown fingered ones. The better your soil is, the better your crops will be. If you manage to create a fertile, healthy and living soil you are already half way there to growing delicious and healthy food for your family.

We might not all be blessed to inherit such a soil but what greater satisfaction could there be than to make your soil fertile for your own benefit and for future generations. The good news is that every soil can be made fertile and the magic ingredient to achieve this is what many people nowadays consider a waste product – compost and manure.

Good compost and manure can revitalise a lifeless soil. It improves the structure, imbibes the soil with life and provides the necessary plant foods. I strongly believe that such a soil will grow vegetables that will feed us properly; it will grow healthy vegetables and hopefully keep us healthy too.

Sir Albert Howard, one of the most influential organic pioneers, states in his Agricultural Testament in 1940:

"The connection which exists between a fertile soil and healthy crops, healthy animals and healthy human beings must be made known far and wide."'

We continuously have to remind ourselves that the top few centimetres of the earth's crust are essential to all higher life on earth. Most old cultures realised this fact and have referred to soil as Mother Earth who provides food for her children.

There is an old country wisdom:

"A farmer should live as though he were going to die tomorrow;
but he should farm as though he were going to live for ever."

We completely depend on the soil for our survival on earth.

Civilisations that have neglected to look after their soil have perished – they simply couldn't feed their people any longer.

On the other hand, some civilisations (China, Japan) have survived for over 4,000 years because they looked after their soils and learned to observe the cycles of nature.

They knew that whatever is taken out of the soil has to be given back in the form of compost or manure. And if we keep doing that our soils will actually get better and better. There is nothing greater we can do than to leave a plot of land more fertile than we found it.

This is what we have to understand: **what we take out from the soil we have to give back!**

This is the difference between growing vegetables or ornamental plants. When you grow vegetables you obviously eat them and so take away the nutrients they have absorbed from the soil. These nutrients have to be replenished every year.

The trouble is that we as a human race are not aware of this. So far, about 2,000 million hectares of soil have been degraded through human activities – that is 15% of the Earth's land area, an area larger than the US and Mexico combined.

Soils can counteract global warming:
Healthy humus rich soil acts as a carbon sink (carbon deposited in the soil) and can thus counteract global warming. Compost contains a lot of carbon. So quite simply: if we use compost in our garden we take carbon out of the atmosphere and deposit it in the soil.

Not even an ounce of bio-degradable waste should be dumped in a landfill site. It should be transformed into the best possible organic fertiliser which will also take the carbon out of the atmosphere.

Life in the soil

It is very difficult for us to fully appreciate what goes on in the soil. If we could only see the creatures toiling away relentlessly we would probably take better care of it.
A healthy soil is teeming with life. They are tiny, but seen through a microscope they open up a fascinating world of wonders. In one gram of soil, the number of bacteria ranges from 100,000 to several billion.

Maybe some figures will impress! In one hectare of good agricultural land (100m x 100m) there are:
20,000kg Micro-organisms
370kg Protozoa
10kg Springtails
50kg Millipedes and woodlice
17kg Insects, beetles and spider
4,000kg Earthworms

All those soil organisms play a significant role in maintaining a healthy fertile soil. If these organisms were not present the soil would have no life – it would die.
Their role is to break down the

crop residues and other natural inputs and mix them with the soil. As they break down the waste, essential plant nutrients are being made available to plants. They are single-handedly responsible for the renewal of life.

And there is another great invention of nature: the warmer the soil, the more active these micro-organisms are and the more nutrients they release. That's also when plants need more nutrients. So how do we encourage these creatures? We simply feed them with compost, manure, crop residues, seaweed, weeds, etc.

To summarise:
A healthy soil produces healthy vegetables, so if your plants are ailing the first question you should ask yourself: is my soil fertile enough?

'The health of man, beast, plant and soil is one indivisible whole; the health of the soil depends on maintaining its biological balance, and starting with a truly fertile soil, the crops grown on it, the livestock fed on those crops and the humans fed on both have a standard of health and power of resisting disease and infection greatly in advance of anything ordinarily found in this country.'
Lady Eve Balfour, Living Earth, 1943.

Know your soil

The soil in your garden may be quite variable. There may be rocky patches where rubble was buried, there may be solid daub good enough for pottery or possibly some excellent dark friable soil which you inherited from days gone by.

Digging Test

In order to identify the most suitable soil for your vegetable garden go out with a spade and dig a few holes around the garden. Usually the places where grass or weeds grow best has the better soil.

A few years ago I was advising a community group who wanted to start an organic market garden. They had already purchased the land and had workers in place keen to get started. The one thing they didn't do was going out with a spade. When I checked the soil it was simply impossible to get the spade into the ground. It was full of rocks. They had to find another site.

You dig out soil the depth of the spade in a few different places and compare the samples. The things to look out for and to compare are:

Colour

Generally speaking, the darker the soil the better it is as darker soils have a higher humus content.

Texture

Is it a sand, silt, clay or peat soil? (see opposite page)

Is the soil loose or compacted?

How easy is it to break a lump of soil? Does it crumble easily or does it stick together? Obviously the easier it crumbles the better the soil.

Are there any worms or worm channels?

We all know that worms are our great helpers and diggers.

Soil profile

Once you have identified a good sample dig a larger hole in this area about 50cm deep and 50cm wide. This will give you excellent information on the depth of your soil. A soil profile is made up of topsoil, subsoil and the underlying rock.

There is usually a clear difference between topsoil and subsoil. The topsoil can be identified by:
- a darker colour
- a looser structure (more crumbly)
- plenty of worm and insect channels
- plenty of plant roots

Plant roots need sufficient depth to grow in. A depth of good topsoil of about 30cm is perfect. However 20cm depth is sufficient but more care and effort is required to improve it.

On some soils there is a gentle gradient from topsoil to subsoil. You won't see the clear distinguishing line between the two layers. These are brown earth soils which are very fertile and free draining.

Soil texture

Over thousands of years rocks have weathered down into small particles which form the main ingredients of nearly all soils. Thus the texture of the soil depends on the physical location and geology of the area.

The texture of a soil is determined by the amount of sand, silt and clay particles present. These are classified according to their size.

Table: Particle sizes:

Sand	0.06 - 2mm
Silt	0.002 - 0.06mm
Clay	less 0.002mm

The proportion of sand, silt and clay present in the soil determines the soil type. Most soils contain a mixture of soil particles. The table below will illustrate what soil texture you have on the site.

Sandy soil:

Soil type	Percentage of:	Clay	Silt	Sand
Sand		10	10	80
Sandy Loam		10	25	65
Loam		20	40	40
Silt Loam		20	60	20
Clay Loam		40	30	30
Clay		60	20	20

How to find out what soil texture you have?

There are two simple ways of determining the texture of your soil:

1. Jam jar test

One rough and ready way of determining your soil texture is to half fill a jam jar with soil, add water until it is about three quarters full, add some vinegar, put a lid on and shake it vigorously for a minute and put it down immediately. The vinegar helps to settle the fine clay particles quickly. The various fractions of sand, silt and clay will separate. The sand and any stones will settle within a minute and will be at the bottom. On top of this is the silt which will settle within a few hours and make up the second layer. The clay particles will take over a day to settle and eventually make up the third layer. The test can be analysed once the water is clear. Any organic matter will be either floating on the surface or on top of the clay bits.

2. Finger test

Take a handful of moist soil and rub it between the thumb and fingers.

Clay soil:

The soil sample is sticky and can be rolled into a ball and sausage shape. The higher the clay content, the thinner the sausage will be.

The soil sample feels gritty and makes a rasping sound when rubbed between fingers. It will not stick together or form a ball.

Silty soil:

The soil sample has a soapy silky feel to it. Sometimes it makes a squeaky sound when rubbed and leaves fingers dirty.

Peaty soil:

Soil sample looks very dark with a spongy feel. It cannot be rolled into a ball.

Characteristics of different soil types

Now that you have identified the texture of your soil you know what the advantages and disadvantages are:

Clay soils are sticky when wet due to poor drainage and can be as hard as rock when dry. They often crack open in prolonged dry spells. Clay soils also take a lot longer to warm up in spring.

On the positive side, clay soils tend to be rich in plant nutrients and leaching of nutrients is less severe than on lighter soils.

A **silty soil** is reasonably moisture retentive and nutrient rich.

However, it compacts easily and can be hard to work.

Sandy soils are very free draining, easy to cultivate and warm up early in spring. The disadvantages are obvious: they can't hold water and nutrients very well.

Loamy soils contain a balanced amount of sand, silt and clay

particles with a fair amount of organic matter. They are the most fertile soils.

Peaty soils (or organic soils) are formed where wet acid conditions prevented the full breakdown of organic matter. They are very rich in organic matter but may be very infertile and acidic, but potentially with a very good structure. They can be made very fertile when properly limed and fertilised.

Drainage and aeration

The combination of bad weather and poor drainage creates great challenges for Irish gardeners. Waterlogged soils take a much longer time to warm up in spring. So be patient and refrain from sowing your crops too early. The soil should be at least 7°C before most crops can be sown and it may be worthwhile buying a soil thermometer.

The main problem of waterlogged soils, however, is that there is a lack of air in the soil. A well-aerated soil is essential for good plant growth and it provides a good environment for the billions of micro-organisms which enliven and improve the soil.

To find out if your soil has a drainage problem simple dig a hole about 30cm x 30cm and fill it up with water. If the water drains away within a few hours you have no drainage problem. If it sits in the hole for a few days you have to remedy the problem.

How can waterlogging be overcome?
- Invest in proper drainage (see diagram below)
- Make up raised beds
- Loosen the subsoil
- Add well-decomposed compost
A combination of the above mentioned methods may work best.

Soil pH
The pH of a soil influences soil fertility. It is measured on a scale known as the pH scale, which ranges from 0-14. A pH value of 7 is neutral, anything below that is acidic and anything above is alkaline. The pH reading reflects the amount of calcium (lime) in the soil. In our wet climate calcium is continually being washed out of the soil often causing acid soil conditions, especially on sandy soils. pH levels can easily be measured with little pH-tester kits available from most garden centres. Most crops thrive well if the pH value is between 6 and 7. If the pH is too low, the following products can be added to the soil:
Ground limestone, calcified seaweed (as Seagreen K or Highland Slag).

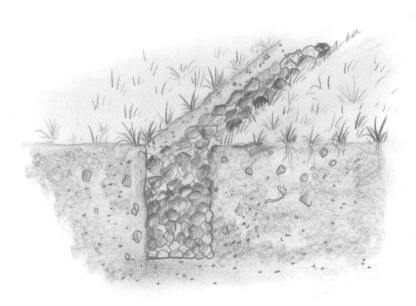

Example of proper drainage

Plant nutrients

Plants absorb the carbon they require from carbon dioxide in the air. All the other nutrients are absorbed as dissolved mineral salts from the soil. The major nutrients that plants require are nitrogen (N), phosphorus (P), potash (K), calcium (Ca), magnesium, (Mg) and sulphur (Su). However, they also require small amounts of so called trace elements which include boron (Bo), molybdenum (Mo), iron (Fe), manganese (Mn), zinc (Zn), copper (Cu) and silica (Si).

These nutrient salts derive naturally from the weathering of mineral particles of the rocks and also through the breakdown of organic matter (compost) in the soil.

Even though nitrogen is abundant in the air, plants can't absorb it. However, plants from the legume family which include peas, beans and clover, can fix nitrogen from the air with the help of soil-borne bacteria (rhizobia). The plants form nodules on their roots which are colonised by the bacteria which, in turn, deposit nitrogen into the nodules which is released into the soil when the plant decomposes.

With an adequate supply of compost or farmyard manure and a leguminous crop (either peas or beans or a clover or vetch green manure) in your rotation you will ensure a well-balanced supply of nutrients as well as improving the structure and, thus, the quality of your soil.

Soil analysis

It is very useful to get your soil analysed to find out its nutrient content. This will give you information on the pH level and nutrient content of your soil.
If the soil analysis shows deficiencies in certain nutrients some of the following organic fertiliser can be used to supplement but never to replace compost or composted manure:
Organic poultry pellets - NPK fertiliser
Rock phosphate-P fertiliser
Calcified seaweed - Seagreen K trace elements + rock potash
Calcified seaweed - Highland Slag - trace elements + rock phosphate + rock potash
Seaweed dust - trace elements
Rock potash—K—fertiliser

Soil structure

The fertility of the soil depends principally on its structure. If the soil is crumbly and can be worked easily, the growing conditions for the plants are favourable. A well-structured soil consists of crumb particles which join the lumps of mineral and organic particles together. The size of the crumbs and especially the spaces between them are very important. Plant roots and soil life need both air and water which are available in these spaces or pores. Poorly structured soils have the tendency to become compact and water-logged.

A good soil structure can be identified by the following parameters:
- Soil smells sweet and earthy
- Soil is relatively easy to dig
- Roots penetrate deeply into the soil
- There is no compacted layer
- There are lots of worm channels
- Topsoil is loose and crumbly (when wet and dry)
- Water drains away easily after rain

How to improve your soil?

A fertile soil is free-draining, slightly acidic (pH 6-6.8), has a good crumbly structure, is rich in nutrients, has a high humus content and plenty of soil life.

To create or maintain a fertile soil use some of the following methods:

Use of good farmyard manure and/or compost
If there are no major nutrient deficiencies in your soil, a decent annual application of compost or composted manure will provide your soil and plants with everything they need. Scientists have recently proven that compost can significantly reduce or minimise pests and diseases in plants.

Use of mulches
It's the method of covering bare soil with an organic material, such as leaf mould, straw, lawn mowings, etc. The advantages of mulching are manifold. Mulching prevents weeds, keeps the soil moist, provides food for micro-organisms and worms and improves the structure of a soil.

Caution:
Mulching the soil around vegetables in wet climates such as in Ireland will provide a cosy home for slugs which are likely to decimate your crops. Mulching is really not advisable in Ireland unless you live in a dry spot and have a very free draining soil. Mulching in winter, however is very beneficial as the heavy winter rains tend to wash out many valuable plant nutrients into lower layers of the soil.

A winter mulch of seaweed is one of the best. Don't worry about the salt, it will dissolve before you plant your crops the following spring. In one garden close to the sea I cover all the beds in October with a seaweed mulch about 20cm deep. In March the seaweed has nearly decomposed with only a few tough bits left. Underneath it the soil is crawling with earthworms –

at least a hundred on each square foot. I carefully put the hard seaweed pieces into the compost and I don't have to dig because the worms did it for me.

If you don't have access to fresh seaweed (it's illegal to collect!) you should either cover your plot with black plastic or with a winter green manure to prevent leaching.

Crop rotation

A well-designed rotation can help improve your garden soil. If you include members of the legume family such as peas and beans – they will fix atmospheric nitrogen and deposit it in your soil. You should also aim to alternate heavy feeders (or greedy vegetables) with light feeders so you don't exhaust your soil. Examples of heavy feeders include: cabbage, potato, leeks and perpetual spinach; light feeders include carrot, beetroot and onion. If you find that your garden has become exhausted, an excellent way for regenerating it is to take out one quarter of your plot and grow a red clover green manure on it every one in four years for a whole year.

Green manuring

Green manures can improve the soil fertility in various ways either by adding atmospheric nitrogen (legumes), by increasing the organic matter content, by stimulating soil life, by preventing nutrients from leaching and by growing into lower compacted layers and thus increasing the rooting depth for plants and bringing already lost nutrients back up again.

Practical points

Should I dig over my garden in autumn?

No. Irish conditions are very different. Instead of frost we get rain in winter. Digging in late autumn is only suited to areas with very cold and dry winters where the continuous freezing and thawing breaks down the clumps and a nice soil tilth is formed. In Ireland the rain washes out valuable nutrients and in our relatively mild winters the weeds will continue to grow. The soil literally turns into mash and becomes waterlogged. In a waterlogged soil all the soil pores are filled with water leaving no space for air. A soil without air is unable to support aerobic life .

How much compost or composted manure should I apply?

It depends on how fertile your soil is. On a fertile soil one bucket of old compost per 2m² should be sufficient to maintain soil fertility. On an average soil 1 bucket per square metre will be enough.

190

On a poor soil 2 buckets per square metre would be required.

Can I make enough compost to feed my vegetables?

The answer is no! You need to supplement with manure, seaweed etc.

When and how often should I spread compost?

Every year you harvest vegetables and thus take nutrients out of the soil, so in theory you need to replenish the soil every year. As you will see in the vegetable section, there are some vegetables that are greedier than others. The less greedy ones such as carrots need very little or no feeding, but if your soil is quite poor they will certainly benefit from an application of very well broken down compost.

Organic fertilisers

If you look around garden centres you will be surprised how many products are labelled as "organic". Probably not many of them are truly organic which means that they are not certified by an organic certification body.

Artificial fertilisers (soluble mineral fertilisers) are banned in organic systems because there is a danger of nutrient leaching into the ground water. A lot of energy is used in the production of these fertilisers and if you force feed your vegetables they are likely to be more susceptible to pests and diseases.

Anyway, the organic mantra is 'Feed the soil, not the plant'. Only bulky inputs such as compost and manures can achieve this.

Organic fertiliser inputs can be divided into bulky fertilisers and supplementary mineral inputs. You will have to rely on the bulky fertilisers and only use the 'supplements' as an additional feed if needed.

Bulky organic fertilisers:

Garden compost
Garden compost is an excellent fertiliser for your garden especially if it is well made. The problem is that you never have enough of it to maintain your soil fertility.

Municipal compost
Fortunately there are now some County Councils and private companies who set up municipal composting plants in order to reduce the waste going into landfill sites. It is well worth finding out if there is one in your area. I get all the compost for vegetable gardens and landscaping from Envirogrind Compost in Pettigo, Co. Donegal. They

produce the best compost and compost mixes I have ever come across.

Cow and horse manure
Both cow and horse manure are excellent organic fertilisers and soil improvers. If you were a certified organic grower you would only be allowed to get manures from animals which are not fed with GM feed. GM soya and maize, however, is in all nuts and mixes. Ideally try to get some manure from an organic farm, but they might not give it to you!
It is advisable to get a load of manure well in advance and compost it well for a few months.

Warning:
In the last few years the Royal Horticultural Society in the UK was inundated with distressed gardeners who had massive crop failures. The plants looked like they were sprayed with a weedkiller.
It was finally found out that the problem was in the manure.
Farmers were using a strong weedkiller to control docks and thistles called Aminopyralid. This chemical went through the cows and horses and ended up in the manure. This chemical was banned in 2009 in the UK. But the chemical will last for at least three years before it degrades. I am not aware of any problems in relation to this in Ireland.

Natural rock phosphate
Only use it if you have a phosphate deficiency in your soil.

Natural rock potash
Only use if your soil is deficient in potassium. Rock potash may take years before it becomes available to plants.

Dolomitic limestone and ground limestone
Use in case of calcium and magnesium deficiency. In other words if you have an acidic soil.

Dried seaweed meal
It supplies many trace elements. Every year I sprinkle some over the garden.

Calcified seaweed
Adds trace elements and calcium.

Poultry manure
Has a very high nutrient content. Even when you compost the manure it is too strong for your vegetables. If you have chickens the best way is to mix it with your garden compost.

Fresh seaweed
Many soils in coastal areas have been made from seaweed and these are still some of the most fertile soils in the country. It really is an excellent fertiliser.
Unfortunately you are not allowed to collect it. You could call the

County Council and ask for permission.

Liquid feeds
Liquid feeds are very popular amongst organic gardeners. They are usually very smelly and unpleasant to use. The nutrients in liquid feeds are generally quickly available to plants thus they are useful as an emergency measure. Comfrey liquid is high in potassium which is especially required for fruiting plants such as tomatoes. Remember liquid feeds are suitable additional organic fertilisers but you can never completely rely on them at the expense of compost or manure.

 Nettle liquid has a lot of nitrogen amongst other nutrients which is useful to give struggling plants a boost. Liquid compost food is a good all-rounder with a good balance of nutrients including trace elements. Liquid feeds are easily made by putting either the leaves or the compost in a water barrel and leaving it to ferment for at least 4 weeks before using it. The liquid should be diluted by 1:10. In the case of the nettle and compost liquid it is easier to manage if the ingredients are placed in a hessian sack suspended in the barrel. The comfrey leaves can be thrown into the barrel. The comfrey variety 'Bocking 14' has the highest potassium content.

Ground Preparation

Getting started

After you have decided on the size and location of your vegetable plot you can mark it out. Place canes or rods at the corners and stand back to look at it and see how it fits into your garden. If you want a square or right angles make sure it is square using Pythagoras's help (ask your children).

Bed preparation – from lawn to garden

There are various options for getting your soil ready ranging from very lazy to really hard work. I would like to discourage you from the toughest method (unless you want to replace the gym for gardening exercise). This is double digging. Many books, especially the older ones encourage you to use this technique but I'm sure it would put many novice gardeners off gardening for life! Double digging is digging over two spits (the length of the spade blade) to a depth of about 50cm.

The use of a rotavator to get your ground ready from grass should also be discouraged as it simply churns up the soil while still leaving most of the shredded grass sods on the surface ready to re-grow within a few days.

So what are our options?

Option 1: Covering with black plastic for 12 months

This is by far the laziest, but very effective method for converting your lawn into a productive vegetable plot. In early spring mow your lawn or strim your meadow and then spread a generous amount of cow or horse manure over the grass (about 1 wheelbarrow for every 3 m²).

After that you cover the whole area with strong black plastic (silage plastic) and secure it well so that the wind won't blow it off. In the following spring lift the plastic, collect the slugs which are stuck to it and you'll be amazed how beautiful the soil is underneath. The only drawback is waiting for 12 months but you can start small in the first year and at the same time prepare a new section for the following year.

Then mark out the beds and path with sticks. The path should be around 40-50cm wide and the beds around 1-1.2m wide. If your

Covering with black plastic:

garden is on a slope you should align your beds going down the slope. The paths will then act as a drainage channel and take the excess water away.

When the soil is dry enough you can start making up the beds. If lots of soil sticks to your boots and tools it's too wet!

You will find that the worms have already done most of the digging and mixing for you during the last twelve months. All you need to do is ruffling up the soil on the beds with a fork and then shovel some of the soil from the paths onto the beds. Let the soil settle for a week (or longer) and then you are ready. Finally, level and smooth the surface of the soil with a rake to make a fine-textured seed bed. The goal is to have finer soil on the top and coarser down below, providing for good water percolation and drainage.

Even if it is still too cold to plant all your vegetables in early spring

you can still prepare all the beds. This will give you a good head start and will also let some early weeds germinate which can be easily raked or hoed off. This will result in far less weeds to appear later on.

Option 2: Single digging

Single digging is a lot harder than just covering but it is great exercise. Never dig if the ground is waterlogged or sticks to your boots otherwise you may cause unnecessary soil compaction. You can either dig in late autumn but then you should cover the plot with black plastic to prevent the nutrients from washing out or you could wait until February/ March. Mark out the plot with a line and take out a trench 40cm wide and about 20cm deep. The soil from this trench should be piled just outside the far side of your plot. It would be beneficial to loosen the soil at the bottom of the trench with a fork and then add compost or manure to it. Then start the second row about 15cm wide and invert the soil into the first trench and repeat the loosening of the subsoil with a fork and compost application. Then you continue with rows 3, 4 etc until you come to the last row. You should end up with a gap into which you can pile the soil from the first trench.

It is very important then to wait for about 4 to 6 weeks before you level the soil and make up the beds. If you try to do this too early you will pull out and expose the sods. You need to give them time to break down.

After that you can prepare the beds as described above.

Example of single digging

Don't let the digging put you off though. It's not the easiest job, especially trying to turn over the sods properly so that the grass won't show. If you find it too tough decide on an easier option.

Option 3: Making raised beds with timber sides

Anyone with even the least carpentry skills can make up a raised bed. The big advantage of this system is that you don't have to dig provided the beds are a minimum of 20cm high. The most suitable timber for this purpose is untreated larch or cedar. They last quite well for a number of years even without wood treatment. Where is the point of growing organic vegetables if the chemicals from the wood preservatives get into the soil and possibly into your vegetables? Avoid using railway sleepers as they are impregnated with the most dangerous chemicals.

The big advantage of this system is that you don't even have to dig the plot over. You can simply place the raised bed over the grass. It's really a great way of converting your lawn into something more productive (see diagram opposite).

Step by step guide
Step 1:
Mark out the area. The width of the bed should be between 1m and 1.3m depending on the length of

your arms. You should be able to reach the middle of the bed without standing on the soil.

Step 2:
Drive in 5cm x 5cm (2"x2") strong wooden pegs about 40cm long at the corners of the bed. The pegs should be sticking out 20cm. If the bed is long you will need extra pegs in the middle.

Step 3:
Screw the planks (20cm high and 5cm thick) onto the pegs.

Step 4:
Lay out thick layers of newspaper (at least 7 sheets) inside the bed onto the grass making sure the newspaper overlaps and covers the whole area.

Step 5:
Place a 5cm deep layer of composted manure on top of the newspaper (omit this step if you plan to grow carrots).

Step 6:
Fill the raised bed to the top with very good topsoil. You may be lucky enough to have spare topsoil in your garden and you could mix that with composted manure from a garden centre. I generally use the Envirogrind compost. They produce a fabulous topsoil mix which consistently grows the best vegetables. It is likely that there are more composting enterprises around the country. These composts would be suitable for mixing in with a topsoil and improve the soil, but they shouldn't be used on their own.

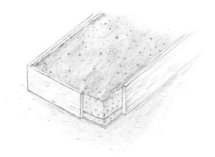

Example of a raised bed

Step 7:
After you have filled the raised beds you should wait for a week for the soil to settle and then you are ready to sow or plant.

There is also an adaptation to this!
My father-in-law made a raised bed on top of his woodshed and he grew delicious onions in it.
In case you don't have a garden you can also made a raised bed on top of concrete or gravel but it should be a minimum of 50cm high.

Warning:
Do not use treated wood or railway sleepers for your raised beds. Pressure treated wood obviously has a longer life-span but is treated with chromated copper arsenate which renders the wood resistant to fungi (copper) and insects (arsenic). There is no point growing your vegetables organically and poison the soil around them. Many studies have

Lazy beds

Lazy beds date back to the early 1800's. They were used by farmers in Ireland who were forced onto poor boggy land where nothing would otherwise grow. Only with the use of lazy beds could they feed their livestock and families.

Anyone who visits the West of Ireland can still see the traces of this ancient cultivation technique which is so unique to Ireland. It is an ideal system of getting a crop out of a very poor and wet soil and secondly lazy beds provide us with an important historical link to the past. I would love to think that every Irish person should get the opportunity to have a go at making a lazy bed once in their life.

We will quickly appreciate that it is not a lazy task. It can be quite back breaking work especially if we don't have adequate tools. At least we don't have to do half an acre of it.

Tools

Each county in Ireland seems to have developed a tool for turning the sods of the lazy beds. A loy is used in many areas for making lazy beds. It is a heavy tool with a large wooden handle and a strong tapering steel blade. The other tools are generally long narrow spades often with a bend in the middle. They were called McMahon spade, Fermanagh spade, Sligo spade etc.

How to make lazy beds?
1. You start off with a lawn. The better the lawn the easier it will be to lift the sods.
2. Mark out the area and stretch garden lines sloping downwards every three feet apart.
3. Place manure on one side of the line about 20cm wide and 5-10cm high. This is on top of the grass.
4. Put the seed potatoes on top of the manure, 20cm apart for earlies, 30cm apart for maincrops.
5. Place the garden line between the two bands of manure and cut the sod with a spade or edging tool.
6. Now comes the tough job. You cut under the sod and turn it onto the potatoes. When you finished the first line repeat this on the other side so the whole drill is covered with sods from either side.
7. After that you shovel some soil from the pathways onto the drills.
8. During the growing season earth up the potatoes once or twice.
9. Harvesting is definitely the best fun: you simply open up the sods (with strong hands and gloves) and the potatoes just lie there on top of the manure which has since decomposed nicely.

Composting

"We can make the sorrow and suffering into a compost, out of which the roses of joy can grow".
-Satish Kumar

Compost is magical stuff.
Composting is a natural process, so even if we make many mistakes it will work out in the end.
Imagine if natural composting (decomposition of organic matter) wouldn't take place, the earth would grow bigger and bigger and we would be living on an enormous rubbish heap.

Composting ensures that all the nutrients which have been taken out of the ground by our crops will return back into the soil. It's a natural cycle, nothing is lost and nothing is gained. This shows how important it is for everybody to compost all their kitchen and garden waste. Every bit that ends up in a landfill site is lost soil fertility. And it's a fact that our soils are becoming more and more infertile.

Tompkins and Bird in their book 'Secrets of the Soil' argue that 'Todays soils are tired, overworked, depleted, sick, poisoned by synthetic chemicals.

Hence the quality of food has suffered, and so has health.
Malnutrition begins with the soil. Buoyant human health depends on wholesome food, and this can only come from fertile and productive soils. Chemical fertilisers cannot restore soil fertility. They do not work on the soil but are enforcedly imbibed by plants, poisoning both plant and soil. Only organic humus makes for life.'

Once people start to compost and they manage to produce black gold there is an incredible feeling of magic and mystery. It really is magical! Just imagine all the smelly, gunky waste, piled up in a heap and very soon – after a few months – it is transformed into humus. If you think about it philosophically it is the end of a lifecycle and at the same time the beginning of new life. It shows that everlasting cycle of death and birth, just outside your house in your little compost bin.
And you should wonder how it happens. It's those billions of microscopic creatures (which we can't even see) who do all the work for us. In fact, in one handful of compost there are more living beings than there are people on Earth!

Composting counteracts global warming / helps to protect the ozone layer!

It's logical if you think about it. Plants absorb (breathe in) carbon (a greenhouse gas) from the atmosphere and when you compost the plants (or anything else) this carbon is going to make up the organic matter or humus which is quite safely stored in the soil for many years and some of it even for many decades. So, the most active way to counteract global warming is to compost every bit of waste which is decomposable. I'm sure that within a decade people and countries will get grants to grow crops for composting which will act as carbon sinks (absorb and store carbon).

What is composting?

Composting is the term given to the natural process by which plant and animal matter is broken down into a rich dark, soil-like material under controlled conditions. This is carried out by a huge range of organisms. Their size ranges from the familiar worm to organisms so small, that they are invisible to the human eye. This natural process is harnessed to deal with our organic waste.

Choosing a site

The place where you make compost should be convenient for you with easy access. Ideally a compost pile should be sited on free draining soil, allowing easy movement of organisms between the heap and the soil.

Collecting the waste

The two main sources of material for composting are kitchen and garden waste. In the kitchen, any uncooked vegetable matter should be collected in a small bin with a close fitting lid, which should be emptied onto the compost heap every few days. Alternatively, collect material to be composted after each meal and add to the compost heap. We usually spread out a sheet of newspaper and wrap the peelings in it before putting it into the compost bin. This way there will be a lot fewer flies annoying you. In the garden, simply add any leaves, grass cuttings or any other organic waste regularly to the pile.

What can I compost?

In general, anything that was once living can be composted. However leftovers from cooked food, meat and chicken etc. can pose problems by attracting vermin.

Choosing a compost container

There is a wide range of compost containers available on the market. It's also quite easy to build your own. In selecting the right container for you, the first thing to consider is the amount of waste you are producing. This obviously varies enormously and depends on the size of your household and the size and type of your garden.

Compost containers come in sizes ranging from 200 litres up to 2,000 litres. Although every household is different, a family of three to four people with a typical suburban sized garden would need a compost bin with a capacity of around 300 litres to meet their needs.

Plastic compost bins

The typical home composting bin available at garden centres or from Local Authorities is somewhat smaller than a domestic wheely bin and has a capacity of around 300 litres. As a rule of thumb, this would be suitable for a household of up to four or five people, but would only be able to deal with a very small amount of garden waste. Bins are filled up gradually over time, so the material at the bottom will always be at a more advanced stage of decomposition having been there longer.

Home made compost bins

If you have a reasonably sized garden, a plastic home composting bin will not be able to deal with the amount of organic garden waste produced. In such a case, a larger container can be fairly easily built using a wide range of materials. Compost bins have been

successfully built using pallets, wood, straw bales, bricks, blocks etc. The key to building your own compost area is to create a place to deposit material which is protected from the rain.

Wormeries

A completely different technique is the use of a wormery to produce compost. This method relies largely on worms to carry out decomposition and does not heat up during the process. A wormery is a fully enclosed container which comes complete with Tiger worms particulary suited to digesting organic waste. The population of worms increases during the process.

Wormeries are suitable for both indoor and outdoor use as they are totally enclosed. They produce top quality compost often used in potting mixtures. They are also very popular with children!

A disadvantage of wormeries is that much more care is needed to ensure that the worms are fed correctly, otherwise the process may be slow or the worms may even die. Wormeries come in a wide range of sizes and types.

Compost tumblers

An innovation in composting is the introduction of compost tumblers. These are drums which sit on a frame and are filled with material to be composted. A handle enables them to be turned regularly and easily, to ensure that air penetrates evenly throughout the compost, and speeding up the process.

New Zealand Box
This is definitely my favourite composting system. It consists of three equal sized compartments. You always put the new material in the first compartment and when it is full you turn the contents from the first section into the middle compartment. You can then start filling the first one again. When it is full again, turn the middle section into the third section and the first one into the second.
It is an absolute fool proof system and you can make brilliant compost in less than three months. It's definitely the best option if you have a reasonably sized garden.

New Zealand Box:

How to make good compost

Composting is not an exact science and everyone can make good compost successfully if you observe the following guidelines.

a) Use the right ingredients - getting the Brown and Green balance right
Making compost is a bit like baking a cake. Compost ingredients can be divided into Green and Brown categories depending on its chemical make-up. In technical terms Green waste contains a high percentage of nitrogen and Brown waste a high percentage of carbon. As a rule roughly equal amounts of each type of waste should be used. Most people find it difficult to gather enough Brown material for composting. A tip here is to gather a few sacks of autumn leaves for addition to your heap throughout the year. But don't be too concerned so long as the (Green/Brown) balance is not too much one way or the other.

When starting a compost heap, first place a layer of brown material in your container. Straw, shredded twigs, paper or autumn leaves are ideal for this. Once this first layer been has placed in the container, Green and Brown material should be added in alternate layers 5cm to 10cm thick from then on. The more varied the ingredients you put into your heap, the better the compost you will make.

The most common problem is that too much kitchen waste and grass clippings are added without enough brown material. This restricts movement of air, which slows down the process, and may cause offensive odours.

Less frequently, problems can arise from the addition of too much Brown material. If too many leaves, twigs, hedge clippings are added the composting process will be very slow.

Green materials (activators):
Grass cuttings
Young weeds
Poultry manure
Comfrey leaves
Seaweed

Neutral materials:
Kitchen scraps
Vegetable peelings
Tea leaves
Coffee grinds
Fruit peelings (only limited amounts of citrus fruit peelings should be used)
Animal manure from non carnivores (sheep, cattle, horses, rabbits)

Brown materials (slow to rot):
Egg shells
Wood ash
Sawdust and wood shavings

Small amounts of soil
Small hedge clippings (either shredded or small twig sized)
Autumn leaves
Old plants
Small quantities of paper (torn up or shredded)
Straw
Hay

Do not add to your compost:

Meat, chicken and fish leftovers
Manure from meat eating animals such as dogs and cats
Certain weeds especially docks, bindweed, ground elder, dandelion, scutch grass
Coal and peat ashes
Glossy magazines
Large woody material
Chemically treated garden waste
Diseased plants
Animal carcasses
Disposable nappies

b) The right moisture content - not too wet and not too dry

It is important that your compost heap is not too wet and not too dry. If too much wet material such as coffee grinds, tea leaves etc. is added, it will restrict the amount of air in the heap, slow down the process and may lead to offensive odours. As Ireland has a high rainfall, it is very important to ensure that your heap is

protected from the rain. All plastic compost bins have a lid, but it is important if making your own compost area to ensure adequate protection from the rain.

A less common problem is a compost heap that is too dry. In this case composting will be very slow as micro-organisms need moisture to work efficiently.

Simply watering the heap should cure the problem.

Micro-organisms thrive in a well aerated environment and so a heap which has plenty of air is much more efficient. A good practice is to stick a garden fork into your compost bin every few weeks and loosen up its contents. This will allow air to penetrate the heap. If you have a larger heap, it is a good idea to turn it every so often. The more often a heap is turned the sooner your compost will be ready. However don't worry! Whilst it speeds up the process, turning your heap is not necessary for the making of good compost.

c) Chop or shred materials if possible

Smaller particles of material are more quickly and easily broken down. For example, a cabbage stalk if added directly to a heap may take up to two years to break down fully. However if shredded or chopped in small pieces the same stalk will be fully composted within a few months.

How do I know when my compost is ready?

The overall aim of composting is to turn household and garden waste into a sweet smelling, dark brown, crumbly compost. When the compost is ready for use there should be hardly any traces of the parent material. Looking at your compost heap will let you know when it is nearly ready for use. If you are unsure, simply crumble it through your fingers. It should be dark, crumbly and sweet smelling if ready. Don't be put off if there are a few woody branches or egg shells which are not fully decomposed. Home produced compost will not typically be as fine as bagged compost available from a garden centre.

How to use your compost

Compost is a valuable addition to the soil and it has a host of uses. Because the volume of household waste shrinks by at least 50% during the composting process, a typical household produces relatively small amounts. Once up and running you will find that you will produce a bucketful of compost from time to time. Even if you are not especially interested in gardening, there will be no difficulty in finding a suitable place that will benefit greatly from a few handfuls of compost.

Mulching:

Spread a layer of about two inches of compost around plants on ground that has been cleared of weeds. This will then suppress new weed growth, improve the soil and hold moisture. This should only be done when the soil has warmed up. Compost can also be used to feed plants growing in containers or pots. Remove an inch or two of the existing soil and replace with a layer of sieved compost. This will lead to a longer life span for these plants.

Soil improver:

Work compost into your soil to enrich it. This is especially useful in the case of vegetable and flower beds. When using compost in this way there is no need to sieve the compost as leaving some smaller twigs etc may even benefit your soil.

Potting mixes:

To make shop bought compost go further add up to 50% of your own compost which has been sieved and mix thoroughly. To make your own potting compost use one part sieved compost, one part sharp sand and one part finely sieved soil and mix well.

Problems which may arise

Offensive smell:

Offensive smells are caused by lack of air because the compost is too wet or too compacted. The solution is to regularly aerate your compost by loosening it with a fork. If this does not work empty the bin and turn the compost whilst adding extra layers of brown material.
Too much green material, especially grass cuttings will also produce a rotten odour. Once again, adding brown material should solve the problem.

Slow break down of material:

A slow rate of decomposition may be caused by adding too much brown material or material which is in pieces which are too large. This sometimes happens in the autumn when leaves and twigs are abundant. Shredding the material or adding more green material will help. Remember that composting takes place at a slower rate in any case in the winter.
Sometimes in the summer your compost heap may be too dry to function properly. As a dry surface may conceal a moist interior double check that lack of moisture is in fact the problem. Dryness can be easily remedied by adding water.

Rats and mice:

A concern that many people have is that a compost area will attract rats and mice. To minimise this problem do not add meat, fish or cooked food to your compost heap. The use of a plastic compost bin with a lid and base will also help. In fact, rats and mice are common in many gardens and a compost heap rather than attracting them may simply become one extra source of food. To avoid problems, it is also a good idea to locate your compost area at the end of the garden rather than beside the house.

Frequently asked questions about composting

Q   **What do I do if there are flies in my compost bin?**

A   The most likely cause of this is that meat, fish or other fatty kitchen waste has been added. Ensure the material is well aerated and add a layer of Brown material.

Q   **Can I compost rhubarb leaves, potato peelings, egg shells, citrus fruit peel?**

A   Yes in all cases. Egg shells will not fully break down but do not be concerned about that.
Potato peelings may sprout but will break down when decomposed. Citrus fruit peel can be added in small quantities. Large quantities may make the compost acidic.

Q   **Should I buy a compost activator?**

A   Generally no. If you want to encourage the composting process simply add a few shovelfulls of old compost or garden soil from time to time.

Q   **Should I add weeds to my compost?**

A   The roots of some perennial weeds should be excluded. In particular docks, dandelions, bindweed, scutch (couch) grass and ground elder should not be added as they are likely to grow throughout your compost. Also do not add any weeds which have seeds as you may end up spreading them throughout your garden.

Q   **Can I compost diseased plant material?**

A   It is not a good idea to add diseased plants to your compost as the temperature in the bin will not be high enough to render them harmless.

Green Manures

Green manures are plants that are grown specifically to build and maintain the fertility of the soil and are always incorporated into the soil. They can be used whenever your plot is unoccupied either over the winter, before a late sown vegetable or after an early crop such as early potatoes. A long-term green manure can be an alternative to compost or manure if it is unavailable.

Benefits of green manures

To prevent leaching:
In nature you will never see bare soil. When the soil is bare it is prone to nutrient leaching or in extreme cases to erosion. A green manure crop covers the ground and makes use of the available nutrients and retains them until the green manure is incorporated back into the soil. While it decomposes, micro-organisms and worms break it down and release the nutrients for the following vegetable crop. Nutrient leaching is a big problem in autumn and winter especially if the soil is still warm and was left bare over winter.

To protect the soil structure:
Green manures protect the structure of the soil especially in areas with high rainfall when the soil tends to become waterlogged and when it dries suddenly and cracks.

To fix nitrogen:
Many green manure crops are in the legume family, they take up nitrogen from the air and fix it in the nodules with the help of rhizobium bacteria.
To feed the soil organisms:
Imagine the work soil organisms are faced with when a green crop is dug into the soil? They will quickly multiply and decompose the residues and release their nutrients.

To break up the subsoil:
Some green manures have strong and deep root system which can penetrate into the subsoil. This loosens and aerates the subsoil so your vegetables have more room to grow. These deep rooting crops will also bring up nutrients which have already washed away, back up to where your vegetables need them.

To control weeds:
It is also believed that green manures are useful in weed control as they smother the weeds.

Unfortunately I have more often seen weeds smothering green manures.

To give the soil a rest:
In traditional farming there was always a fallow period in the rotation to give the soil a rest so it can recover from continuous cropping. During the fallow period the ground got quickly covered with weeds, including leguminous weeds such as clovers and vetches. Instead of leaving it to chance you could take one section out your rotation and grow a long-term green manure for the whole year to build up the fertility of your soil.

How to grow green Manures

Sowing:
Prepare a good seed bed and broadcast (sprinkle) the seed over the bed at the recommended seed rate. You then rake the seeds into the soil. If you have weedy ground you can also sow them in rows to allow for weed control between the rows.

Incorporating the crop:
A green manure crop is best incorporated just before flowering. You shouldn't let it go to seed as all the plants' energy is put into seed production and this diminishes the value of the green manure. Also you don't want to create a new weed problem.

It is best to mow or strim the crop a day or two before digging it in. You can also consider using a rotavator to incorporate the crop but some green manures such as ryegrass may survive and become a problem for the follow on crop.

It is very important to let the green manure fully decompose before sowing or planting your crop otherwise seed germination is inhibited. You should wait for at least 4 weeks before sowing.

Green manure plants

Green manures can be divided into legumes and non-legumes or long-term and short-term crops. In the following list I only include the ones which I have grown in Ireland.

Legumes

Field beans:
Field beans are excellent nitrogen fixers and are extremely hardy. They can be sown from late September until late October and still produce a good ground cover over winter. November sowings, however, will only give you a moderate ground cover in the winter. A huge advantage of field beans is their ease of incorporating them into the ground.

White clover:
White clover is not suitable as a

quick crop. It really needs to be in the ground for a whole year to show its benefits. The best use for white clover is to undersow it with tall crops such as sweetcorn, kale or Brussels sprouts. There has been a lot of scientific research done on this. Apart from fixing nitrogen, researchers have found a massive reduction in common brassica pests if they were undersown with white clover. That's how you do it: you broadcast the clover seeds in April onto a fine seed bed and plant your vegetables into the clover in mid May after clearing a small space for planting. The white clover needs to be cut at least twice during the growing season so it doesn't compete too much with your crops.

Red clover:

Red clover is the best nitrogen fixer of all. It also needs a long growing season. The best use for red clover is to sow it after an early harvested crop such as early potatoes in July. It can then stay over the winter months and incorporated into the soil in early spring. As it has fixed large amounts of nitrogen it should only be followed by greedy plants such as the brassicas, leeks or perpetual spinach. If you want to give your garden a rest, this is the ideal plant. You can sow it in early April. In this case you will have to mow or strim it a few times, leaving the mowings on the ground.

Alsike clover:

Alsike clover is a very attractive crop which is suitable for poorer and more acidic soils.

Crimson clover:

Crimson clover has a more upright growth with the most attractive crimson-coloured flower heads. It really is an amazing sight but in terms of nitrogen-fixing it is much inferior compared to red clover.

Trefoil:

Trefoil is another excellent nitrogen-fixing green manure. It is very easy to grow and is suitable for undersowing (see white clover).

Winter Vetch:

Winter vetch is what many people in Ireland know as the wild pea even if it is not closely related to it. It is usually grown in a mixture with other green manures such as ryegrass. It should be sown in mid September until early October. It covers the ground well and fixes a moderate amount of nitrogen.

Non-legumes

Many of the non-leguminous green manures belong to the brassica family. While they are suitable for farming, their use in vegetable gardening is very limited as you will find it hard to fit them into your rotation. If you grow any brassica vegetables, you had better stay away from them. Brassica green manures include rape, stubble turnips, fodder radish, mustard.

Phacelia:

Phacelia is definitely my favourite green manure. It does not fix nitrogen but it has a deep fibrous root system which can quickly make use of all the available nutrients. It is also one of the most attractive looking and wildlife friendly plants. Studies have shown that phacelia attracts large numbers of slug predatory ground beetles. It also attracts masses of hover-flies that eat aphids and bees, hence the German name for it: Bienenfreund (bee's friend).

Phacelia is a very quick crop which can be sown from spring until late summer anywhere you have a gap for a few months. Hard frosts will kill the plant, but I have seen it over-winter on a number of occasions.

Buckwheat:

Buckwheat is another very attractive green manure with the same uses and sowing dates as phacelia, but for some reason I have never managed to get a good cover from it.

Grazing rye:

This is a very strong and reliable green manure. It grows extremely well over winter from a September sowing. It is usually sown in a mixture with winter vetch. Beware though that it doesn't become a weed in the following year. It really has to be dug in thoroughly otherwise it might re-grow again.

Earthworms

Worms were described by Aristotle as the **'intestines of the soil'**, they could also be considered its vascular system, since, when they are lacking, soils get hard-packed as if their arteries had hardened.

Earthworms are our best friends. They tunnel their way through our garden soil and mix soil with plant residues to produce the most important substance on Earth: **humus.**

Worms improve the soil by:

- aerating the soil
- improving the waterholding capacity of the soil
- improving the rooting of plants as they grow into the worm channels
- improving the structure of the soil
- bringing up plant nutrients from lower levels of the soil
- loosening compacted ground
- making those nutrients available to plants
- mixing soil particles with organic matter and thus prevent them from leaching (washing out)
- having a neutralising effect (pH)

Earthworms transform plant and animal residues into available plant food. Worm casts (droppings) contain five times the amount of nitrogen, seven times the amount of phosphate and eleven times the amount of potassium than the surrounding garden soil.

How to encourage worms into your garden:

Worms would already be in your garden if the conditions for them were right. So it is not advisable to introduce worms to a 'wormless' garden as they may not survive.

To increase the worm population in your garden and make your soil more fertile consider the following:

- Worms prefer neutral soil (pH around 6.5 to 7). If you carefully lime an acidic soil with either ground limestone or calcified seaweed this will significantly improve the living conditions for worms.
- Avoid excessive soil cultivations especially rotavating. After a few years the worms will do the digging for you and you may just have to loosen and aerate the soil with a fork.
- Feed your worms with compost or composted manure.

Rotation

Crop rotation was used by many traditional farming cultures throughout the world. If crops are grown continuously on the same piece of land the soil will sooner or later become exhausted. When people had the chance to move on to a new area this was fine as the natural vegetation quickly settled in again and restored the soil. When there was no longer an option of moving on, people had to look after and care for their soil for survival. Any rotation was designed to local soil and climate conditions and they always included a fallow period which allowed weeds to grow and replenish the soil.

Crop rotation was abandoned when people had access to artificial fertilisers to keep up the nutrient supply to plants but as we will find out, nutrients are not the only thing that a soil needs.

What is a crop rotation?

The principle of crop rotation is to group related vegetables together and move them around your garden so that they do not grow onto the same plot for a number of years.

What are the benefits?

The use of crop rotations has various benefits:

Pest and disease control:
Pest and disease pathogens can build up to catastrophic levels if the same host crops are grown on the same spot year after year. If you move your crops around you interrupt the cycles of those pests and diseases. Don't think that crop rotation is the cure for all pests and diseases. Unfortunately this is not the case. Rotation is only effective for soil-borne pests and diseases that are specific to a particular plant family.

Do you think a slug would mind if it has a lettuce or a radish for breakfast? The carrot fly will find your carrots no matter where they are in your garden.

However, crop rotation is absolutely essential in limiting the spread of the following soil-borne pests and diseases:
- Clubroot on brassicas (cabbage family)
- Nematodes on potatoes
- White rot on alliums (onion family)

Soil fertility:
Vegetables differ in what they take out of the soil and what they give back to it. If you include peas and

beans in your rotation they will add nitrogen to the soil. A leguminous green manure in your rotation will add even more.

On the other hand if you grow only heavy feeders such as cabbages your soil may quickly get tired.

Soil structure:

A well-designed rotation can help in improving the structure of your soil. Some crops have a very deep taproot which can penetrate into the subsoil and extract nutrients from low down. Thus you should alternate deep-rooting vegetables (or green manures) with shallow rooting ones.

Weed control:

If you alternate weed susceptible crops such as onions with weed suppressing crop such as potatoes or cabbages the weed problems for the susceptible crops may be lessened.

How long should the rotation be?

A three-year rotation is the absolute minimum and suitable if you have only three beds available. Obviously the longer the rotation is, the more benefits you get from it. A four-year rotation is usually sufficient and easily managed. If it suits your needs you can have a much longer rotation.

Step by step guide to planning your rotation:

1. **Make a list of all the vegetables you want to grow**. Make sure that haven't included vegetables that can't be grown outdoors in Ireland (cucumbers, tomatoes, peppers, aubergines) and don't include perennial vegetables such as asparagus in this list. Perennial vegetables have to be grown a permanent plot.

2. **Group the vegetables into plant families**. You will find a list of vegetables and their botanical families on the following page.

3. **Divide up the garden into equal plots**. If you have decided on a four-year rotation you divide your vegetable garden into four equal plots.

4. **Decide which families will be grouped together**. You will notice that there are more than four vegetable families. The families should be suited to each other; for example the carrot and onion family is very compatible because they have a similar growth habit.

5. **Draw** up a plan.

Vegetable families

Please note: the vegetables in brackets cannot be included in your rotation. They are either perennials or just not suitable for the Irish climate.

Brassicaceae (Cabbage family)
Brussels sprouts
Broccoli
Cabbage
Calabrese
Cauliflower
Kale
Kohlrabi
Pak choy
Rocket
Radish
Swede
Turnip

Leguminosae (Pea family)
Pea
Bean

Solanaceae (Potato family)
Potato
(Tomato)
(Pepper)
(Aubergine)

Umbelliferae (Carrot family)
Carrot
Celeriac
Celery
Florence fennel
Parsnips
Annual herbs: dill, coriander, chervil, parsley

Compositae (Daisy family)
Chicory
Endive
Jerusalem artichoke
(Globe artichoke)
Lettuce
Salsify
Scorzonera

Alliaceae (Onion family)
Garlic
Leek
Onion
Scallion
Shallot

Chenopodiaceae (Beetroot family)
Beetroot
Chard
Spinach

Cucurbitaceae (Cucumber family)
Courgette
(Cucumber)
Marrow
Pumpkin
Squash

Unrelated vegetables
Sweetcorn
Corn salad
Winter purslane
(Asparagus)

Companion Planting

I really risk being confrontational about this subject. I know that many vegetable gardeners strongly believe in companion planting when a plant either 'loves' or 'hates' another.

Companion planting is the practice of planting more than one crop in a bed. It is thought that one type of plant is either beneficial or harmful to the neighbouring plant either by keeping insect pests or diseases away or by inhibiting or improving the growth of neighbouring plants due to the aroma they release.

As a result there are many companion planting charts and posters available to gardeners. However, there is very little scientific evidence to support this fact. The combinations I tried were highly unsuccessful. The most common companion planting association is to grow a row of carrots next to onions. Apparently the smell of the onions keeps the carrot root fly away and the smell of carrots should keep the onion fly away. It really did not work for me – the carrots were still riddled with the fly and the onions never got onion fly anyway.

One scientific experiment tested the effects of six companion plants (marigolds, nasturtium, pennyroyal, peppermint, sage and thyme) which were each grown in association with cabbage. The cabbage was sampled weekly for eggs of common cabbage pests. There was no reduction in pest number as a result of the treatments.

You should take these charts with a pinch of salt and give them some entertainment value rather than believe in their accuracy.
There is definitely a need for more experiments to identify any potential benefits from companion planting.

Intercropping

Intercropping or interplanting are alternative words for companion planting but there is no claim that one particular plant will harm or benefit a neighbouring plant unless it is scientifically proven. It is an excellent way of maximising your garden space and just the fact that there is a greater plant diversity, there is probably less likelihood of pests and diseases getting out of hand.

There are various ways for mixing vegetables in a bed:

Row intercropping
Grow a different vegetable in each row at the same time. For example, instead of having four rows of parsnips in a single bed you could sow alternate rows of parsnips and beetroot.

Mixed intercropping
Grow two or more different vegetables in a bed at random or in mixed patterns. This can have a beautiful effect and it gardening fun.

Relay intercropping
Grow fast growing vegetables between slower growing widely spaced crops. For example you can plant lettuce or radish between kale and Brussels sprouts. The lettuce and radish will be harvested before the bigger plants need that space.

Intersowing
I'm not actually sure if this term exists, but you can mix seeds of vegetables which germinate and mature quickly with vegetables that germinate slowly and also mature more slowly. The best example is to mix a few radish seeds in with your carrot seeds. The radishes will germinate very quickly and show you where the row is so you can hoe. The radishes can be harvested well before the carrots need that space.

Examples of fast growing vegetables which are suitable for planting in between slower crops:

Lettuce - especially loose leafed types or dwarf varieties.
Radishes – but remember they are in the brassica family so be careful not to confuse your rotation.
Turnips – they are also brassicas so, only suitable for intercropping with other brassicas.
Oriental salads – excellent for intercropping as they can be harvested at any stage.
Annual spinach – one of the best intercrops as you can harvest it even at the baby leaf stage. The biggest benefit is that it is not susceptible to any specific soil-borne pest or disease, so you don't have to worry about your rotation. It's a very flexible crop.

Examples of slow growing vegetables which have space at their early stages:

Brussels sprouts
Kale
Sweetcorn

Warning-Spacing:
It may seem obvious but it deserves a mention: intercropping doesn't give you an excuse to cram

plants together. For example if you intercrop parsnips and beetroot you can't just sow beetroot between two rows of parsnips; you have to substitute one row of parsnips for beetroot.

Shading:
When you mix vegetables select them carefully to avoid shading and excessive competition for water and nutrients.

Once you start experimenting you can have lots of fun and make more discoveries.

Catch cropping

Catch cropping refers to making use of the ground either before or after it is needed by the maincrop. For example, early potatoes may be harvested in July and they can be followed by a catch crop of turnips, Chinese cabbage, Florence fennel or oriental salads. Also late planted crops such as kale, Brussels sprouts, leeks and purple sprouting broccoli can be preceeded by a quick maturing catch crop such as lettuce, radish, turnip, annual spinach or oriental salads.

The three sisters

Perhaps the best historical example of intercropping is the "Three Sisters" in which corn, beans, and squash are planted together. Native Americans throughout Mesoamerica developed this system to provide food for a balanced diet from a single plot of land. Each of the crops is compatible with the others in some way. The tall corn stalks provide a support structure for the climbing beans. The beans do not compete strongly with the corn for nutrients and fix additional nitrogen from the air. Squash provides a dense ground cover that shades out many weeds which otherwise would compete with the corn and beans and lessens water evaporation from the soil.

Sowing

Seed requirements for good germination

Viable seed:
Seeds must have been fertilised and contain a living embryo. They deteriorate in storage. This affects the amount of seeds that germinate, the germination time and also the vigour of the seedlings. On average, seeds store for 2-4 years in a cool, dry place. Parsnip and celery seeds, for example, last only for one season. Seeds should never be left in a hot or damp polytunnel as they will deteriorate quickly.

Correct temperature for germination:
Each crop has got its minimum, optimum and maximum temperature for germination. Generally, the higher the temperature the better the germination. On the other hand, too high a temperature can be detrimental (e.g. lettuce does not germinate well above 25°C). An ideal average temperature for most crops would be about 18 - 20°C.

There are different types of heated propagation units-
- Benches with soil warming cables on sand and thermostat.
- Heating pads with thermostat.
- Electrical propagators
- Home-made unit using insulating material and electrical heat source, i.e. light bulbs.

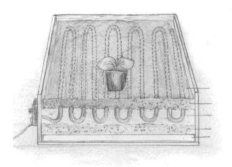

Example of a heating bench

Moisture and air:
Seeds need moisture and air to germinate.
They need to imbibe 40- 50% water for germination to take place. The higher the temperature the higher the water uptake will be. If there is too much water in t h e soil/compost:
- temperature is lowered
- availability of air and water is decreased
- fungal diseases are encouraged.

Light:

A few vegetable seeds require light to germinate, i.e. lettuce, celery. Once germination has occured, all plants require light to photosynthesise. In winter and early spring, the natural light levels are quite low, so artificial light may be necessary to prevent plants from becoming drawn (leggy).

Seed storage:

Most vegetable seeds will keep easily for the next growing season provided they are kept cool and dry (exceptions are parsnips and celery). Never leave seed packets outside in the garden, in a polytunnel or in a damp shed or garage, because the high humidity will quickly ruin them. An air-tight glass jar or a ziplock bag is an ideal storage container. Seeds should be kept dry and stored at low temperatures. They should ideally be kept in your coolest room, or better still, in a fridge. Apart from parsnips and celery I use started seed packets for two or at most three years and then buy new seeds. I'm aware that many seeds will keep for much longer but I find that the vigour of the plants decreases with age and thus the quality of vegetables will decrease as well.

If you want to be a perfectionist you can buy silica gel from a chemist and place it in a separate open-topped container in the glass jar with your seed packets. The silica gel will absorb the moisture from within the glass jar. The silica gel is blue when dry and turns pink when moist. When it has turned pink you can dry it in an oven for a couple of hours and then put it back into the jar. Seeds kept under such ideal conditions will keep substantially longer.

Sowing methods

In theory all vegetables can be sown directly into the ground where they are to grow, and thinned out to their final spacing.

1. Direct sowing

When sowing into the garden soil ensure that the soil is loosened deep down and that the top surface of the soil is very fine and flat so that the tiny seeds won't fall down between the clods.

Generally speaking root crops such as carrots, beetroot, parsnips, swedes, turnips and radish don't transplant well and are therefore sown directly into the ground. Transplanting those crops may cause forking of their taproots (especially in carrots). Also vegetables with large seeds such as peas and beans are generally sown direct (to save space in the propagation house).

Seeds can also be pre-germinated before sowing out into the ground. Most other vegetables will perform much better if they are raised indoors and planted out at a later stage.

2. Transplanting

Many gardeners nowadays prefer to start their vegetable plants indoors in a glasshouse or south-facing windowsill. After hardening off, these transplants are planted out into the garden. The process from sowing to planting out may take about 4 - 10 weeks depending on the season and the crop. Most vegetables (excluding root crops) benefit from transplanting because:

- there is a more uniform plant stand in the plot,
- easier weed control as plants are weeks ahead of the weeds,
- it shortens the growing period in the garden so allowing more crops to be grown on the same land than could be achieved by sowing directly into the soil,
- transplanting is also used for plants whose seeds are too difficult to germinate in the garden (e.g. celery, which has tiny seeds).

The main disadvantage of transplanting is that the plant roots can get damaged during planting. The plants could suffer because the leaves lose water through transpiration and it can't be fully replenished by the roots. The plants suffer until new roots are produced.

This transplanting shock is a big problem with bare root transplants but not so much with modular transplants.

Types of transplants

A. Bare root transplants:

Seeds are sown directly into a seedbed in a polytunnel, cold frame or outside in a sheltered spot and planted out into their final position six to ten weeks later. This is the traditional way of raising certain plants, especially crops like leeks, cabbages, kale, Cauliflower and Brussels sprouts.

Advantage:

- Cheapest way of transplant raising (no cost for trays)

Disadvantages:

- Poor germination and poor plant stand compared with other methods
- Not suitable for early plant production, because extra heat is necessary for successful germination
- There may be pests and diseases in the soil of the seedbed
- Slow establishment of transplants due to extensive root damage (up to 50% of roots may be lost)

B. Blocks:

Blocks are frequently used by commercial growers and hobby gardeners.

Advantages:

- there is very little root disturbance
- blocks are easy to handle
- there is no competition from other seedlings when planted

out
- early production is possible if there is additional heat

Disadvantages:
- needs a lot of space
- takes time to produce the blocks
- uses a lot of compost
- slower to plant than modules

C. Modular or cell trays
Modular trays are becoming the most popular method of transplant raising. There are now many different types of plastic trays available with different numbers and sizes of modules (also called cells or plugs). There are some good quality trays available which will last you for many years but also some very cheap and quite useless ones.

Advantages:
- good crop establishment
- uniform plant development
- faster transplanting, thus reducing labour requirement

Disadvantages:
- relatively high cost of trays
- a high degree of management skills required to produce quality transplants in cells with a very limited volume of compost to hold nutrients and water

Example of modular trays

Sowing depth
Seeds need a good contact with the soil so they need to be sown in drills and covered with soil.

However, if the seeds are sown too deeply they may not have enough reserves to be able to reach the surface of the soil. On the other hand if seeds are sown too shallow, the germinating seeds are more likely to dry out.

Small seeds only have small reserves and should be sown shallow.

Example of a cold frame

221

Example of a cloche

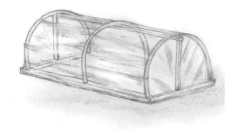

Successful transplanting

When vegetables are planted out from a cosy warm place indoors and have to face the cold and the wind they will certainly struggle to survive.

Hardening off

Plants that are raised indoors must be acclimatised before they are planted outside. It's like a weaning process. The easiest method is to put them in a cloche or even better a coldframe. A coldframe is simply a box with removable glass or clear plastic lids. The plants should stay in the coldframe for about a week prior to planting out. Every day during the week open the glass a bit more than the previous day until on the last day when it is completely off day and night.

Transplant early

Don't let your transplants get pot-bound in the modules and don't let your bare-root transplants get too big. Younger seedlings establish a lot better with little or no check to their growth. Modular transplants should be planted as soon as the root ball comes out easily without the compost falling off it. The longer you leave them after that the more stressed they get.

Transplant in dull weather and in the evening

If you plant out your seedlings in the morning on a beautiful hot sunny day they are likely to wilt due to extensive evaporation.

Seed composts and nutrient requirements

Germination will take place without any nutrients - indeed better than with nutrients. However, seedlings require a balance of the main nutrients (N, P, K) as well as trace elements to sustain plant growth for a short period. High levels of nitrogen will inhibit germination and may even damage the roots of seedlings. As the plants develop they require more nutrients for their growth. When the seedlings are potted on, a richer compost should be chosen or alternatively liquid feeding will be necessary to sustain healthy plant growth.

A good seed compost should be free draining and well aerated. It should also have a fine texture.

Sources of organic compost:

There are now various suppliers of organic seed and potting composts. There are even some organic peat-free composts. Do ensure though that these are certified organic composts.   Unfortunately it is still legal to call a non-organic compost 'organic' even if it is not. This also applies to fertilisers such as poultry pellets, so if you are in doubt please ask the supplier who the organic certification body is and the relevant certification number. If there isn't one it is not really organic.

The following table shows an overview of my preferred sowing method for each vegetable. This is only based on my own experience, other gardeners may prefer different methods. You will soon find out what works best for you!

Vegetable	Preferred sowing method	Number of seeds per cell	Sowing depth (in cm)	Time sowing to planting (wks)
Bean, Broad	Direct Sown		5	
Bean, French	Direct Sown		4	
Bean, Runner	Direct Sown		4	
Beetroot	Direct Sown		1.5	
Broccoli, Sprouting	Transplant	1	2.2	4-5
Brussels Sprouts	Transplant	1	2.2	4-5
Cabbage, Chinese	Transplant	1	2.2	4-5
Cabbage, all	Transplant	1	2.2	4-5
Calabrese	Transplant	1	2.2	4-5
Carrots	Direct		1.5	
Cauliflower	Transplant	1	2.2	4-5
Celeriac	Open tray, then prick out	Broadcast, then 1 per cell	1	8-10
Celery	Open seed tray, then prick out in modular	Broadcast, then 1 seedling per cell	1	8-10

Vegetable	Sowing method	No. of seeds per cell	Sowing depth (cm)	Time from sowing to planting
Courgette	Sow in 7cm pots	1	2	4wks
Endive	Transplant	1	1	5wks
Fennel, Florence	Transplant	1	1.5	5wks
Garlic	Direct Planted			
Kale	Transplant	1	2.2	4-5wks
Kohlrabi	Transplant	1	2.2	4-5wks
Leeks	Transplant	2	1.5	7-8wks
Lettuce	Transplant	1 (or 4 for leaf production)	1 (surface)	3-4wks
Onion (from sets)	Direct			
Onion (from seeds)	Transplant	4	1.5	7-8wks
Parsnip	Direct Sown		1.5	
Pea	Direct Sown		3.5	
Radish	Direct Sown		2.2	
Rocket, Salad	Transplant (or direct)	5	1.5	3-4wks
Spinach, Annual	Transplant (or direct)	4	1.5	4wks
Spinach, Perpetual	Transplant (or direct)	1 (thin to one)	2	4-5wks
Squash	Transplant	1 seed per 7cm pot	2.5	5wks
Swede	Transplant	1	2.2	4-5wks
Sweetcorn	Transplant	1 seed per 7cm pot	3.5	4-5wks
Swiss Chard	Transplant (or direct)	1 (thin to one)	2	4-5wks
Turnip	Transplant (or direct)	1	2.2	4wks

Tabe: Germination temperature for vegetable seeds

Crop	Germination temperature in °C			Days to germinate (at optimum temp)
	Min	Opt	Max	
Beetroot	8	28	33	6
Broccoli	7	25	30	4
Brussels sprouts	6	30	33	4
Cabbage	10	30	35	4
Carrot	7	25	30	8
Cauliflower	8	23	30	5
Celery	15	20	24	7
Cucumber	20	30	35	3
Kale	10	32	37	4
Leek	8	25	30	7
Lettuce	7	18	23	3
Onion	10	23	33	7
Parsley	10	23	30	13
Parsnip	10	17	20	14
Pea	15	23	27	6
Pepper	18	30	37	8
Tomato	5	27	33	6
Turnip	15	30	38	3

Harvesting and storing

When to harvest vegetables

Artichoke, globe
Globe artichokes produce ripe heads in July and August. They should be harvested when they are still green and tightly wrapped. They should be used within a few days after harvesting. They can also be frozen.

Artichoke, Jerusalem
Harvest the tubers from October onwards. They can be left in the ground over winter and harvested when required.

Asparagus
You can start harvesting in the third year after planting. Harvest the spears when they are about 15-25cm above the ground but before the heads open. Cut the spears off at the soil line or just below. Stop harvesting if the spears get thinner. The maximum harvesting period is about 6 to 8 weeks.

Bean, broad
Harvest the beans when the pods are fully developed and the seeds are large enough but still tender. They should be picked on a weekly basis. If you have too many they can be frozen.

Bean, runner and French
Harvest the pods before they are full sized. Younger beans taste a lot more tender. You can expect your first harvest about 3 weeks after the first flowers have appeared. Don't allow the beans to mature on the plants or bean production will decrease substantially. If you have a glut you can freeze the beans for use in winter.

Beetroot
Harvest when the roots are about 8 to 15cm in diameter or smaller if you use the thinnings. The main-crop beetroot for storage should only be harvested in October. They can then be stored in boxes of sand until the following April.

Brussels sprouts
Harvest Brussels sprouts before the buds open. Always pick the lower sprouts first. To speed up the ripening you can remove the cabbage-like head, which is delicious in its own right. Brussels sprouts can be frozen.

Calabrese
Harvest when the flower head is fully developed but before the flowers begin to open. Cut 15cm below the flower head. After cutting the main head the smaller side heads will develop. These should be cut on a regular basis. Calabrese can also be frozen.

Cabbage

Harvest when the heads are firm but before they split open. Early varieties are more likely to split than winter ones. The flavour of savoy cabbages improves after frost. Dutch cabbages should be harvested in late October and stored in a shed.

Carrot

Harvest the roots when they are about 3cm in diameter or smaller if you use the thinnings. If you want to store the carrots leave them in the soil until October. Pull or dig them out carefully without damaging them and twist off the leaves. They can be stored in boxes of sand until April.

Cauliflower

Harvest when the heads are firm and full sized but still white and smooth. Once they are ready they will not last long in the garden as the curds open up and begin to flower. If you have too many at a time you can pull up the plants and hang them upside down in a cool shed or garage. They will last for a couple of weeks. Alternatively they can be frozen.

Celeriac

Harvest the roots as required from October until November. You can then lift the remaining crop, remove the leaves and store in boxes of damp sand in a cool shed.

Celery

Harvest when the plants are about 30cm tall. Once they are ready they may last about two to four weeks in the garden before becoming stringy. Once cut, they will last for about a week in a plastic bag in the fridge.

Courgette

Start harvesting courgettes when the fruits are about 10cm long. Harvest at least twice a week. They are best if used fresh.

Fennel, Florence

Harvest when the bulbs (swollen stem bases) are about 10 to 15cm in diameter. This happens usually about 6 to 8 weeks after planting out. The leaves can be used as a flavouring or as a garnish. If you have too many you can store the bulbs (leaves cut off) in a plastic bag in the fridge for up to 2 weeks. Florence fennel can also be frozen.

Garlic

Dig out carefully when leaves have turned yellow but before they fall over. Dry the bulbs thoroughly and store in a cool, dry place.

Kale

Harvest the lower leaves in autumn as required. Regular harvesting of the lower leaves increases the health of plants. Kale leaves keep for a week in a plastic bag in the fridge.

Kohlrabi

Harvest when the thickened stem is about 10cm diameter (the size of a tennis ball). The autumn crop can be harvested in October. You should trim the leaves and roots and store in a cool, dry place. They will keep for about two months.

Leek

With the proper choice of varieties you can harvest fresh leeks from July until March. Harvest them as required as they don't store well.

Lettuce

Start using lettuce as soon as the first hearts form. Once ready in the garden they will quickly bolt. Always grow small quantities at regular intervals to reduce wastage. If you harvest early in the morning they will keep much better. If placed in a plastic bag in a fridge they will keep for a week.

Onion

Harvest onions when most of the leaves have fallen. Loosen the roots with a fork and two weeks later pull out the onions and spread them out in the sun or in an open shed to let them dry. When completely dry you can tie the onions in bunches with a string and store them in a cool, dry place.

Parsnip

Harvest the roots from mid October onwards until early spring. Frost tends to improve the flavour. They can be left in the garden and used as required or if your garden is too wet in winter they can be stored in boxes of damp sand in a cool shed or garage.

Pea, garden

Harvest when the pods are fully developed and still tender but before seeds develop fully. The seeds can be frozen.

Pea, sugar snap

Harvest when the pods are fully developed but not yet stringy. They can be frozen.

Pea, mangetout

Harvest when the pods are still flat and not stringy. If you have too many you can freeze them.

Potato

Harvest new potatoes as needed from July onwards. Only dig out what you need on a weekly basis as they continue to grow and don't store.

Harvest maincrop potatoes in October and store in boxes of damp sand or in a clamp. Only store healthy tubers that are not damaged.

Pumpkin

Harvest pumpkins for storage when the skins have hardened enough. Harvest before the first frost. They can be stored in a cool, frost-free shed for about three months. Leave the handles on the fruit otherwise they are more likely to rot.

Radish

Harvest summer radish as required. Never sow too many at the same time as they quickly bolt once mature. Winter radishes can be harvested in October. You should twist off the leaves and store in boxes of damp sand.

Salsify and scorzonera

Harvest the roots from October onwards. They are best left in the ground and used as required as they are very hardy. Harvest them carefully as the roots snap easily.

Squash

Harvest summer squash when the fruit is young and tender. Winter squash should be harvested when mature, shortly before the last frost. They can be stored in a frost-free shed for a couple of months.

Swede

Harvest the roots when required from early autumn until spring. They can be left in the garden over winter or stored in boxes of sand in a shed.

Sweetcorn

Harvest when the kernels are completely filled and in the milk stage. Use your thumbnail to determine this. The silks should be dry and brown at this stage. They can be frozen.

Turnip

Harvest when roots are 5 to 10cm in diameter. They should be harvested regularly as older turnips become stringy. The autumn maturing crop can be stored in boxes of sand for a couple of months.

Storage of vegetables

Storing fresh vegetables:

Most fresh vegetables keep best in a plastic bag in the fridge. Don't store ripe fruit in the same compartment as they produce ethylene gas which may cause yellowing of green vegetables, russet spotting on lettuce,

toughening of asparagus, sprouting of potatoes, and a bitter taste in carrots. You should remove the tops of root crops and remove excess soil. In case of green vegetables (salads, spinach) they should be harvested early in the morning. Immediately bagged and refrigerated.

Storing in the garden:

The following vegetables are frost hardy and can be left in the soil throughout the winter and used as required up to early spring when they will start to grow again and become woody. It is beneficial to earth up exposed parts of the roots with soil or cover the beds with straw held down by netting. But be aware that a straw covering may increase the slug damage to your crops. However, outdoor storing is only recommended if your soil does not become waterlogged over winter. In this case you may be better off storing them in boxes of damp sand.

Examples include:

Carrot
Celeriac
Parsnip
Jerusalem artichoke
Swede

Storing at room temperature:

The following vegetables can be stored at room temperature but out of direct sunlight:
Garlic, onion, shallots.

Storing loose in a cool but frost-free shed:

Some vegetables can be stored on wooden racks in a shed or garage or alternatively placed in net bags and hung up.

Examples include:

Firm Dutch winter cabbage

Swede

Storing in boxes of sand in a frost-free shed or garage:

This is by far the most reliable way of storing root vegetables over the winter months. In some years they will last until May the following year. Any container will do – wooden boxes, plastic bins etc. Simply alternate layers of damp sand with vegetables. If the vegetables don't touch each other diseases spread more slowly. A lid is recommended to keep out potential vermin.

Some guidelines:

- Only store vegetables that have sufficiently matured in the garden. Mid-October is the best time to lift the crops.
- Never store damaged or diseased vegetables (eat them first!).
- Never wash root vegetables if you want to store them. It is sufficient to rub them clean. The surrounding soil layer protects the roots.
- Keep the sand moist.
- Check the contents every month and discard diseased vegetables.

Examples include:

Beetroot

Carrot

Celeriac

Jerusalem artichoke

Parsnip

Potato

Swede

Storing in clamps:

This is the traditional storage method in Ireland. It is a useful way of storing your root crops over winter if you don't have space under cover. You do have to be aware of rodents, though. Clamps were traditionally placed outdoors but they work even better in a shed or barn.

How to make a clamp:

Place a free draining material at the base of the pile (rushes or sand about 20cm depth).

Stack your root crops in a pile on top of it with sloping sides, with the largest roots at the bottom. The width at the base should be around 60cm and the height of the finished clamp around 60cm high. Cover the pile with 20cm of rushes or straw and then with a 15cm layer of soil.

Examples include:
Potato
Carrot
Parsnip
Celeriac
Swede
Beetroot

Freezing vegetables:
In summer you may often have gluts of vegetables and freezing is an easy way of preserving a wide range of vegetables. It's important to harvest them when they are at their best stage for eating and process them immediately. They should be prepared in the same way as if you would use them for cooking.

Then they must be blanched before freezing. The word blanching may be confusing here as it also means excluding the light through earthing up with soil or covering crops. Here, blanching refers to boiling vegetables for a short period of time before freezing.

To blanch vegetables you bring a large saucepan of lightly salted water to the boil, then put the prepared vegetables in a wire basket or large sieve and dip them into the boiling water for the recommended time period (see below).

You then lift out the wire basket and place it in a large bowl of cold water for a couple of minutes. Drain the vegetables and dry them on a towel. You can then put the vegetables in freezer bags or boxes and remove as much air as possible by sucking the air out. It's advisable to label the bags with the name and the date. They should keep well for up to a year.

Blanching times:

Artichoke, globe	5 mins
Asparagus	3 mins
Bean, broad	3 mins
Bean, runner	2 mins
Broccoli and calabrese	4 mins
Brussels sprouts	4 mins
Fennel, Florence	3 mins
(cut into 3cm chunks, freeze in rigid container)	
Peas	2 mins
Sweetcorn	5 mins

Weeds

The term 'Weed' doesn't always apply because if plants grow in their natural area - in a forest, field or along a path they an important part of the natural vegetation. Many of them can be eaten (nettle, chickweed, ground elder, dandelion etc.) and/or have medicinal qualities. The mineral content of the weeds is surely beneficial for the soil. Weed compost also makes a brilliant soil improver. We should be more grateful to our weeds as valuable compost ingredients.

Weeds play an essential role in nature by covering bare soil as quickly as possible to protect the soil from erosion or leaching of nutrients.

The definition of a weed is 'a plant growing in the wrong place' or 'a plant that competes for nutrients, light, air and water with the crops you want to grow'.

Weeds fall into three categories, annual, biennial and perennial weeds:

Annual weeds complete their life-cycle from seed to seed within one year. Some annuals can even complete several lifecycles in one year. These are called ephemerals. Annual weeds are the most troublesome in your garden. They have adapted to the frequent cultivations in your vegetable plot. They are even dependent on you to prepare a nice seedbed for them. They could not survive in a permanent meadow or lawn. The problem of annual weeds may increase every year. The first years after starting from a green field site you will have relatively few annual weeds but once they manage to spread their seed, they are unstoppable.

Common annual weeds:
Chickweed (*Stellaria media*)
Shepherd's Purse (*Capsella bursa-pastoris*)
Groundsel (*Senecio vulgaris*)
Hairy bittercress (*Cardamine hirsuta*)
Fat hen (*Chenopodium album*)
Speedwell (*Veronica* spp.)
Mayweed (*Matricaria perforata*)
Field Pennycress (*Thlapsi arvense*)
Common Fumitory (*Fumaria officinalis*)

Biennial weeds complete their lifecycle from seed to seed in two years. These weeds have not really adapted to vegetable garden conditions. As they require two years to mature any soil disturbance during this time will destroy them. Biennial weeds are only a problem (but only a minor problem) in your fruit, herb or ornamental garden which does not get as much attention as your vegetable plot.

Common biennial weeds:
Burdock (*Arctium* spp.)
Hogweed (*Heracleum sphondylium*)
Ragwort (*Senecio jacobaea*)
Garlic mustard (*Alliaria petoliata*)
Teasel (*Dipsacus fullonum*)

Perennial weeds last for more than two years. Many of them are extremely difficult to get rid of. They are great survivors. Their survival techniques include underground storage organs from which they can regenerate if the plant is killed (lesser celandine), low lying rosettes which escape the mower (daisy, plantain), the capacity to regenerate from small root sections possibly from a rotavator or from digging (dock, dandelion).

Perennial weeds will certainly be your biggest problem in the first year of your garden but once you have got rid of them they are a far lesser problem than annual weeds. The only trouble is they are hard work to get rid of in the first place.

Common perennial weeds:
Coltsfoot (*Tussilago farfara*)
Comfrey (*Symphytum officinalis*)
Creeping buttercup (*Ranunculus repens*)
Creeping thistle (*Cirsium arvense*)

Dandelion (*Taraxacum vulgaris*)
Daisy (*Bellis perennis*)
Dock (*Rumex* spp.)
Field bindweed (*Convolvulus arvensis*)
Ground elder (*Aegopodium podagraria*)
Horsetail (*Equisetum* spp.)
Lesser celandine (*Ranunculus ficaria*)
Nettles (*Urtica dioica*)
Plantain (*Plantago* spp.)
Silverweed (*Potentilla anserina*)
Scutch or couch grass (*Elymus repens*)

Indicator plants

Wild plants can give you a good idea of how good your soil is, as they have adapted themselves to certain site and soil conditions. They are thus known as **indicator plants**.

Wild plants have the purpose of balancing and even improving soils. For example, thistles (*Cirsium arvense*) with their hollow stalks and roots bring air into the soil; thus they improve compacted soils where they prefer to grow. Nettles (*Urtica dioica*) prefer to grow in nutrient rich soils, especially near any kind of dumps and leave behind a very dark, fertile and humus rich soil. The coltsfoot (*Tussilago farfara*) with its large leaves grows well in wet, compacted soils. Its large leaves 'pump' water out of the ground.

Good fertile humus soil:
Chickweed
Cleavers
Common fumitory
Common mouse-ear
Creeping thistle
Fat hen
Field pennycress
Groundsel
Red deadnettle
Redshank
Speedwell
Stinging nettle

Wet soils with poor drainage:
Coltsfoot
Comfrey
Creeping buttercup
Horsetail
Rushes
Silverweed
Water Mint

Well aerated, but moist soil:
Chickweed
Corn spurrey
Forget-me-not
Fumitory
Red dead nettle
Speedwell

Acid soil:
Horsetail
Pansy
Plantain
Sorrel

Alkaline soil:
Charlock
Coltsfoot
Cornflower

Common poppy

Compacted soil:
Creeping thistle
Docks
Great plantain
Ribwort plantain
Pineapple mayweed
Silverweed

Weeds: friend or foe?

Weeds are only a problem if they grow close to your vegetables and **compete for water, nutrients and light**. This can cause a substantial loss in yield. Some vegetables with sparse foliage are more likely to be overrun with weeds. You will notice that your onions, carrots and leeks need a lot more weeding than crops with a better shading effect such as broad beans, cabbages and potatoes.

Another problem with certain weeds is the fact they may **harbour pests and diseases** which may later spread on to your vegetable crops. Examples include weeds in the brassica family such as shepherds purse which may spread various brassica pests and diseases. Weeds may also **encourage fungal diseases** by restricting the air-circulation around the vegetables. As Irelands cool damp weather is already a major contributor to fungal diseases you should be extra vigilant to remove weeds especially in crops which suffer from fungal diseases. By keeping those crops weed free and the soil around them lightly hoed you will substantially reduce the risk of blight on potatoes and mildew on onions. Weeds make harvesting a lot more difficult especially if you have prickly weeds like thistles and nettles. You also have to be careful when you grow oriental salad vegetables and use the cut-and-come-again technique for harvesting as some weeds may sneak into the plants and while some of the weeds are edible and sometimes even delicious (chickweed, hairy bittercress), others are poisonous (foxglove, groundsel, nightshade).

Apart from all the real disadvantages, weeds also make your vegetable garden look less attractive.

The value of weeds

Weeds are not always bad. They don't always compete with your vegetables and don't always harbour pests and diseases or encourage fungal diseases. Some of them are not invasive and taste quite nice in a salad.

In fact, weeds have also some beneficial aspects: they protect bare soil and prevent erosion, they can provide a diverse micro-climate and ecosystem as many of them may be food plants for other creatures. Their roots also help to improve the biological activity and structure of the soil.

The importance of hoeing!

Without weeds I would have very little reason to hoe and without hoeing half the pleasure of gardening would be gone. This seems a little exaggerated but it's true. Any time I hoe I have a smile of satisfaction on my face because I know how much my vegetables benefit from it. When you hoe on a dry, sunny day you leave the weeds lying on the ground. This encourages the multitude of soil inhabitants to break them down and release the nutrients back to your crop. Through hoeing you will also create a nice tilth through which water and air can penetrate easily. This tilth is just like our own skin and we surely do not want our pores clogged up!

In order to maintain this tilth you should gently hoe the soil around your vegetables at least every two weeks. The weeds are there to remind you!

Weed control

Changing the soil conditions:
After having identified the importance of weeds as soil indicators we can, to a certain extent, change the soil conditions and thus make it more difficult for certain weeds to thrive. If, for example, your soil is wet and compacted you are likely to encounter weeds such as creeping buttercup, rushes, dock and plantain. If you improve the soil

by loosening the compaction and improving the drainage those weeds will find it a lot more difficult to establish. Similarly if you increase the pH level of an acid soil, weeds such as sorrel or horsetail might be less of a problem in the future.

The weeds which thrive in fertile healthy soil, however, will have to remain with you.

Rotation design:

The design of your crop rotation will have an effect on weeds. In order to minimise the weed problem it is recommended to alternate weed suppressing vegetables with weed susceptible crops. Weed suppressing vegetables are generally strong growers with a large leaf cover. Examples include, cabbage, kale, cauliflower and potatoes. Weed susceptible vegetables have very little leaf cover and weeds can compete with them easily.

Examples include onion, carrot, scallion and leek.

Rotation design for weed control:

Year 1: Cabbage / cauliflower
Year 2: Onion / leek
Year 3: Potato
Year 4: Carrot / parsnip

Compost and manure management:

Compost heaps and manure piles may be sources of weeds, both seeds and roots. If you manage to make a hot compost by frequent turning of the heap you may possibly achieve a temperature of 60°C which is enough to kill most weed seeds and roots. This is however very rarely achieved on a small compost pile. So you should be careful what weeds you put in. If you weed before the plants flower there is obviously no danger.

The compost I buy in from Envirogrind is turned ten times and it reaches a temperature of close to 70°C making it completely weed free.

While manure is an excellent organic fertiliser you are often introducing new weeds (docks and rushes) into your garden. It is advisable to get a pile of manure at least three months before using it and turn it once or twice.

Planting density:

It is often recommended to space your plants a little bit closer so that the soil is covered more quickly and thus preventing weeds from germinating. This may be counterproductive in Irish conditions which are ideal for fungal diseases (humid, mild). If you want to lessen fungal diseases such as potato blight or mildew on onions you should space those crops a little bit further.

The use of transplants:

If you raise your plants in modular trays they are between 4 to 6 weeks old before you plant them out into the garden. They are way ahead of the weeds. During this time you can use the stale or false seed bed technique.

Stale seed bed technique:

Ideally the seedbed should be prepared a few weeks before you intend to sow your crops. The ground preparation and raking will stimulate new weeds to germinate. These can easily be controlled through raking or shallow hoeing in dry weather. The more often you do this the more weeds can be controlled before you actually sow or plant a crop. The most efficient use of this technique would be to flame weed the weeds prior to sowing or planting. The reason for this is that it doesn't disturb the ground as a hoe would do and thus no new weeds are stimulated into growth.

Green manuring:

The use of a green manure crop is supposed to suppress weeds as otherwise bare ground is covered with a crop. In my experience green manures are excellent for improving the soil but one thing they didn't do for me was controlling weeds. Quite a few times my green manure crops got overrun by weeds, especially if it was broadcast sown.

Growing under mulches:

This method is frequently used by organic growers, especially for wider spaced crops such as courgettes and pumpkins, but is also used for many other crops such as onion and garlic.

There are various materials available:

Mypex (lets air and water through, but not weeds)
Recycled paper mulches
Natural mulches (leafmould, composted bark, composted wood chippings, etc)

The plants grow through the holes of the mypex which is either cut or burnt with a hot steel bar. It's a very effective way of weed control, limiting handweeding to only a very small area.

Personally I like to see what's going on in the soil and I love hoeing too much. I only once used a ground cover to grow cabbages. This was a complete failure as nearly every transplant was eaten by slugs. But don't let this put you off. There are many gardeners who successfully use this method of weed control.

Natural mulches also act as an excellent soil improver but unfortunately are quite unsuitable for most Irish gardens as they generally house and feed large populations of slugs. If you have a low slug population in your garden, it is well worth a try.

237

Practical tips:

- Hoe on dry sunny days and hand weed when the ground is wet. When hoeing on a hot day the weeds can be just left on the ground to decompose.

- Never hand weed where the hoe can reach, only hand weed around or between plants.

- Hoe or weed when the plants are small as it is so much faster.

Recommended tools:

I honestly would be lost without my two hoes – the oscillating hoe and the round hoe. The oscillating hoe is the easiest hoe to use. You simply swivel it along the ground. The round hoe (or draw hoe) is excellent to get weeds from underneath cabbage or lettuce leaves. For larger gardens you can buy a wheel hoe, but it's only worth it if you cultivate at least half an acre. There are also various flame weeders available, but they are rarely used in small vegetable gardens.

> *"A man of words but not of deeds*
> *Is like a garden full of weeds"*
> - Anonymous

Keep your garden healthy

The aim of organic gardening is to provide a healthy garden by creating a fertile living soil, increasing biodiversity in your garden and implementing a suitable crop rotation. All emphasis should be placed on preventing pests and diseases rather than having to react to them. In fact, once a pest or disease establishes itself on your crops there is often very little you can do to control it effectively. Protecting your plants from pests and diseases begins long before the crops are sown or planted in your garden.

Your vegetables don't get attacked for no reason, and you can be like a detective identifying the possible causes.

Definition:
Diseases are caused by fungi, bacteria and virus.
Pests are caused by creatures bigger than the ones above.
Disorders are problems caused by environmental conditions such as mineral deficiencies, extreme temperatures etc.

We will find out what makes plants ill and what keeps them healthy.

What makes plants ill?
When plants become diseased or riddled with pests it is often not accidental. If the right plants grow in the right conditions in good earth it is very unlikely that there will be any trouble.

Climate
No gardener can change the climate in the garden. We have to adjust the growing techniques accordingly. There is absolutely no point in working against it.

- In high altitudes with frequent late frosts it is pointless to grow early vegetables or early flowering fruit trees. They become weak and thus susceptible to pests and diseases.
- In cold and wet areas (such as Leitrim) it is impossible to grow warmth loving crops such as tomatoes, cucumbers, peppers and aubergines outdoors.
- Exposed sites near the sea or other open areas can cause a weakening of your plants. Leafy vegetables will suffer whereas root crops are alright.
- Heat and drought (very unlikely in Ireland) have also a negative and weakening effect on your plants.

239

Micro-climate of your garden

The climate within your own garden can be quite different than the climate outside your perimeter, if for example you have a high hedge growing around it and it is south-facing. This will protect and shelter your garden from strong winds.

Water

Without water there would be no life on earth. If there is too little water available for plants they will suffer and too much water can cause fungal diseases and slows down plant growth.

Soil

It's very simple: a healthy soil produces healthy plants and a poor soil produces poor plants.
The soil is the home of your plants. They are connected to the soil with their roots and spend all their life there. A poor soil can cause many problems to plants because they can't escape.

Nutrient deficiencies or nutrient overload

It is obvious that plants with a well-balanced 'diet' can grow much stronger and healthier than others which are force fed with 'junk food' or starving.
As with people, if plants don't get enough 'food', they become weak and ill, but problems also occur if they get too much of some nutrients. This will cause soft lush growth which is much more appetising for many pests and diseases.

Pollution

Luckily there is still very little air pollution in Ireland, except in some built up areas, near busy roads or factories. Many of the pollutants are heavy metals and can be transported by the air. When plants absorb them they can cause disturbances in the growth of plants.

What keeps your plants healthy?

Soil fertility - a healthy soil produces healthy plants

The care of your soil is the most important duty of every gardener. It is the most effective method of preventing a pest or disease outbreak. The ideal soil is a loose, moist humus rich soil full of worm and other soil life with a balanced nutrient content, including all the trace elements. It may take a good few years to achieve this, but even the poorest soil can be made very fertile using organic methods.

Biodiversity

A garden with good biodiversity (the sum of species in a given area) is a lot less prone to sudden attacks of pests and diseases as there is a balance of pests and predators.

240

To increase the biodiversity in your garden is probably one of the most rewarding pleasures in gardening as you have the opportunity to create habitats and homes for many living creatures that have been pushed to the edge either through the destruction of their habitats or chemical poisoning.

It is very easy to create diverse habitats in your garden and there are many excellent books that describe in detail how to do it.

Beneficial habitats include:
- Pond
- Log or branch pile
- Dry stone wall or stone pile
- Native hedgerow and include fruiting shrubs
- Native trees
- Clump of nettles in the corner of your garden
- Wildflower patch

Apart from creating specialist habitats you can also increase the biodiversity within your vegetable patch through:

- Crop rotations - where pests and diseases are eliminated by prolonged periods without their hosts.
- Polycultures by growing different crops next to each other (inter-cropping) or undersowing with a green manure crop (under-cropping).
- Variety mixtures- by growing different varieties of the same vegetable in a plot. This technique has been very successful with potatoes and lettuce and there is a lot of scope for further experiments.

Hygiene
Hygiene in and around the vegetable garden is very important for pest and disease control. This includes weed control and the removal of damaged or diseased leaves or plants from the garden. If your vegetable garden is messy it is much easier for pests and diseases to spread much faster. Your wildlife areas should be positioned a fair distance away from your plot as the beneficial creatures usually travel further and faster than the pests.

Good seeds
You should always start with good and clean seeds. They should always be stored in a cool, dry place and not for too many years. I usually keep seeds for only two years and then buy new ones. New seeds are a lot more vigorous.

Healthy transplants
The same applies to transplants. It is very rare that all transplants in a tray are of the same quality and you should only plant the best. There is no point of starting a plant hospital.

Right plant, right place

Plants that are not suited to your climate and soil conditions will never thrive and therefore will be the first ones to be attacked by pests and diseases. In Ireland you can't grow good cucumbers or tomatoes outside. Some may survive and you may even get a few ripe tomatoes on it if you grow them on a south-facing wall in a sheltered garden somewhere in the south or east of the country. However, the same plant may produce a hundred fruits if grown in a polytunnel.

Resistant varieties

If you find that every year your parsnips get canker and your potatoes blight you should consider using a variety that is resistant or tolerant to the relevant pest or disease.

Examples:

Potato: Sarpo Axima, Sarpo Mira, Orla and Setanta are very resistant to blight

Pea: Hurst Greenshaft is very resistant to mildew

Parsnip: Gladiator F1 and Javelin F1 have some resistance to canker

Lettuce: Dynamite is resistant to aphids

There are many more examples and you will find them when you browse through seed catalogues. Unfortunately it is often claimed that there are carrot rootfly resistant carrots available. They are sold with very appropriate names such as Flyaway F1 and Resistafly F1. When I grew them my carrots were still riddled with the dreaded fly and apart from that, they tasted horrible.

Timing of sowing

You can sometimes avoid outbreaks of pests and diseases by adjusting your sowing or planting dates. The best example is to sow your carrots in late May or early June. This avoids the first generation of carrot rootfly in May. Another example is to sow your peas only in mid April to avoid foot rot disease.

Breaking the cycle

You could have brassicas (cabbage family) growing in your garden all year round. This makes it very easy for all pests and diseases to survive and re-infect new crops. I always clear my cabbage patch in mid January and only plant the first brassicas again in early May. I'll never get nice spring cabbage but at least I hope to get fewer problems.

Adjusting the spacing

If plants are spaced too closely they are a lot more susceptible to fungal diseases such as grey mould or mildew. If you want to lessen any potential problem you can always space your crops a little bit further apart. This increases the airflow through the crop and reduces the incidence of fungal diseases that thrive in more humid conditions.

Proper sowing and planting

Good care should be taken when sowing seeds and planting vegetables. The better they start off the more likely they will do well.

Managing pests and disease

Whilst many pest and disease problems can be prevented, there are various occasions where pest or disease numbers increase to such high numbers that they can cause serious damage to your crops.

It is crucial to properly identify the culprits. It happens often that an innocent bystander who happens to be at the scene is accused of the act. It may have been the one who has just eaten the culprit.

Mechanical control

Netting

Mechanical controls include barriers that keep pests away from your crops. There are various types of netting available to protect your vegetables (fleece, crop covers, bionet, bird netting). It's important that you use the right type of netting for the relevant pests. A net to keep the small carrot root fly out needs to be a lot finer than a net for cabbage white butterflies.

Collars

Collars are used around brassicas to prevent the cabbage root fly from laying its eggs near the cabbage stems.

Traps

Many pests can be lured into traps. The beer trap for slugs is a popular example. If you use this method ensure that the lip of the container is above the soil surface otherwise you may also catch some ground beetles which would have eaten many more slugs than you have caught. Personally I can think of a much better use of beer!

You can also buy yellow sticky tape from garden centres to catch flying pests such as aphids. They are very good as indicators to find out which pests you have but they will not control pests sufficiently.

Handpicking

Handpicking larger pests such as slugs, leatherjackets or caterpillars can be quite efficient especially in a small garden. I know some gardeners who get great satisfaction from this.

Biological control

Biological control includes attracting beneficial creatures that feed on pests as well as introducing predators for the job! These predators can be purchased by mail order but are generally very expensive especially for a small area.

It is much more efficient (and a lot cheaper) to attract native beneficial creatures into your garden than to purchase foreign species.

Examples of natural predators include:
Hoverflies - the larvae and adult hoverfly feed on aphids.
Lacewing – feed on aphids
Ladybirds – feed on aphids
Beetles – feed on slugs and many other small pests
Earwigs – most people believe they are pests but they also feed on aphids
Frogs – feed on slugs

Chemical control

There are a number of so called 'safe' organic sprays available to the gardener. They are safe in the way that they are fully biodegradable within a couple of days (with the exception of copper sulphate) but nearly all of them will also kill beneficial insects and thus disrupt the natural cycles.
The garlic spray (Envirorepel) is one exception. It only masks the smell of host plants so that pests find it less attractive or get confused. Apparently it also strengthens the plants so that they become more resistant.

A milk/water spray (1 part milk and 7 parts water) was probably the best new discovery in organic disease control. I have successfully used it to control diseases such as grey mould and mildew on a variety of vegetables. You can spray it with a little plant spray directly onto affected plant parts ideally three days in a row and the disease stops spreading further. Unfortunately it didn't work for potato blight.

Other organic sprays include:
Derris – to control aphids, caterpillars, flea beetle
Pyrethrum - to control aphids, caterpillars, flea beetle
Insecticidal soap – to control aphids, whitefly, spider mites
Soft soap – to control aphids
Quassia – to control aphids, apparently safer than derris and pyrethrum
Bluestone (Copper sulphate and washing soda) – to control potato blight, apple scab
Sulphur – to control powdery mildew, rose blackspot

Note: All these sprays can also damage beneficial insects or can be harmful to fish, livestock and worms (i.e. Bordeaux mix)

Home-made sprays:
Home-made sprays are often prepared by hobby gardeners to control various pests and diseases. They are illegal in the EU as they are not tested. Some of them are

extremely toxic (rhubarb spray) to all sorts of wildlife. The most interesting spray is a **compost tea** or extract. You soak one part of compost with ten parts of water for about a week and stir it daily. You then dilute it with another 10 parts of water before spraying it onto susceptible crops to prevent or halt fungal diseases. Many scientists all over the world achieve tremendous results in controlling a large variety of diseases. But remember you are not allowed to make it yourself.

Common pests

Rabbits and hares
Both rabbits and hares can be a serious problem in your vegetable garden. However they can be easily kept out of your vegetable plot with a rabbit proof fence.

Birds
Most birds are very beneficial to your garden as they consume many pests including slugs. But sometimes they can also cause some damage. Early in spring crows and other large birds may peck out your onion sets, pigeons may eat your young cabbage plants and most birds will love any fruit you grow.
If you find that you have a recurring problem, simply put a bird net over the crops you want to protect.

Aphids

Aphids are one of the most common pests in any garden. There are many different species, often adapted to just one or two host plants. They feed by sucking the sap out of plants and thus weakening them and making them more susceptible to fungal diseases. They also transmit virus diseases from one plant to another. Aphids are a lot more common in sheltered gardens. In exposed gardens they are often blown away from your vegetables.

Cabbage caterpillars

Caterpillars of the cabbage white butterfly are one of the biggest nuisance for everybody who tries to grow brassicas.

Leatherjackets

Leatherjackets are the larvae of the crane fly ('daddy long legs'). They feed on the roots and stems of many different plants causing considerable losses of young plants, especially lettuce. It is believed that leatherjackets are only a problem in new gardens but this is certainly not the case in Ireland. Even well established vegetable gardens suffer from this most annoying pest.

There is no other organic control than to handpick the larvae. The only times you can find them is when you prepare your ground or after it has just nibbled through the stem of your newly planted lettuce.

As soon as you notice a small lettuce plant wilting, pull it out and carefully search the soil around and you will find the culprit. You can also try to trap them by placing a layer of lawn mowing on the ground and cover this with thick cardboard or black plastic. After two days you can check the trap and dispose of any larvae.

Cutworms

Cutworms are the caterpillars of various moth species. They are usually grey or brown, quite fat and up to 4cm long. They live just under the soil surface and feed on root vegetables, brassicas and lettuce. As with leatherjackets they often sever the stem at ground level and they can also be found near affected plants.

Millipedes

Millipedes have two pairs of legs per segment whereas the beneficial centipedes have only one pair per segment. There are many different types of millipedes and they may sometimes damage seedlings. I have never experienced them as being a major problem so I leave them in peace.

Wireworms

Wireworms are the larvae of the click beetle. They are thin, orange-brown larvae about 2cm long with a hard body and three pairs of legs near the head. They kill seedlings by feeding on young stems and roots. They can also tunnel through potatoes and carrots. They are a problem in new garden and after a few years they will decline. I'm not aware of any organic control method apart from hand picking them whenever you come across one when digging.

Common diseases

Plant diseases are a lot more difficult to identify than pests. Diseases are caused by fungi, bacteria and viruses and are very difficult to treat organically. The best organic spray is the milk and water mixture as mentioned above. The best method in dealing with diseases is to avoid them in the first place. If a plant becomes diseased there is often something wrong in the environment or in the soil. A good gardener should try to identify where the problem lies rather than reaching for a cure that may create even more problems in the future.

Botrytis (grey mould)
This is one of the most common plant diseases which affects a wide range of plants. The symptoms are white-grey fungal growth on affected areas. It is difficult to control so keep your garden clean and remove any diseased leaves as soon as you notice them.

Mildew
Powdery and downy mildew are also common problems for many vegetables. Powdery mildew can be a serious problem on courgettes. Downy mildew is a serious problem for onions especially during wet summers.

Potato blight
Potato blight is covered in detail in the potato section.

Rusts
Rusts may affect various plants but in particular the allium family. There are now varieties available that have some resistance to it. Rust doesn't kill the plants, it reduces the yield and makes the vegetables unsaleable.

Slug Control

'Whenever I see a slug on a piece of lettuce,' Grandma said, *'I gobble it up quick before it crawls away. Delicious.'*
-Roald Dahl

Slugs are definitely the most hated creature in gardens. Nearly every gardener has a nightmare tale about them. However, slugs are an important part of the food chain in your garden. They help with the decomposition of organic material and are an important food source for birds, beetles, hedgehogs, frogs and toads.

Many natural gardeners give up their organic credentials when it comes to slug control and unwillingly bring out a packet of slug pellets. These slug pellets are partly responsible for the decline in birds and other slug predators.

And remember, slugs have been on this planet millions of years before us and will probably outlive us!

Slugs originated in the sea so the moist Irish conditions are a slug heaven compared with the warm dry summers of central Europe. This explains why slugs do most of their damage during the night though they are also active during dull rainy days.

Natural predators

Slugs and snails are an important food source for many animals. The more predatory animals we manage to lure into our garden, the more balanced and harmonious it will be.

Birds

Many birds enjoy a sluggy snack. Amongst the best ones are thrushes, starlings, magpies and seagulls.

Hedgehogs

Unfortunately hedgehogs are becoming rarer, possibly due to unwise use of slug pellets by hobby gardeners. However we can try to create habitats and save havens for hedgehogs in our organic gardens by piling up leafmould under shrubs or we can create artificial habitats for them making a pile with branches, leaves and other garden residue. There are even hedgehog houses for sale.

Frogs

It is a great idea to create a wildlife pond in your garden to encourage frogs. They are excellent slug predators. They hide in hollows of stone walls, thus a dry stone wall near a pond will create an ideal habitat for frogs.

Beetles and other small predators

Carabid beetles are important slug predators as they share a similar habitat with slugs and feed on their eggs and even on young, small slugs. Also spiders and centipedes will feed on slug eggs.

Ducks

Many gardeners are convinced that keeping a few ducks in the garden will almost certainly minimise even the worst slug problem. I used to keep a pair of ducks in a half acre walled garden with thousands of lettuces and the ducks would go on slug patrol up and down the rows of lettuces picking out the slugs from under the lettuce leaves but never touching the plant itself. It is thought that Khaki Campbell ducks and Indian Runner ducks are the most suitable for the job. If you decide to keep ducks you will need to provide them with a paddling pool.

Chickens

Chickens are also very effective in controlling slugs. They would, however, eat or scratch out all your vegetables. But if they are let into your vegetable patch once all the crops are out they will do an excellent job in controlling slugs.

Biological control

The slug predator is a nematode called *Phasmarhabditis hermaphrodita*. The product name is 'Nemaslug'. It is applied with water and the beds are watered with it.

Garden design for slug prevention

In order to encourage the above mentioned slug predators we need to create a garden which is as natural as possible. The garden should contain some of the following features:

- Native, wide hedgerows where birds can breed undisturbed and have an alternative food source.
- Wild corners where stones, branches, leaves are left for hibernating hedgehogs and many other beneficial insects.
- A wildlife pond which attracts frogs and toads with a stonepile near it.

However, the area directly around the vegetable plot should be a little less naturally designed. Wide paths, ideally gravel or slabs, around the plots will make it more difficult for slugs to visit your plants. Secondly grass paths are suitable around your plots. The grass would need to be mowed regularly and the clippings collected in a box.

So hopefully, after having left wild areas and habitats on the edges of your garden the slugs may be quite happy to stay there, especially if they have to cross wide gravel paths to get to your goodies.

Cultural control

Mulching

Slugs will thrive in a nice mulch layer around your plants. They absolutely love it. Unfortunately (given all the soil benefits of mulching) I really think that mulching your vegetables is fatal to do in Ireland.

Composting

Slugs are naturally attracted to your compost bin. And that's fine. They are doing their proper job there. They break down dying plant material and produce humus. The only thing is, you don't want them to come out of the compost and visit your garden at night so it would be wise to create a barrier (gravel path) between your compost area and your vegetable plot or site your compost area a fair distance away from your vegetable plot.

Preventing Access

Barriers with materials spread around plants

Materials which absorb moisture from slugs as they cross it, stops them from going on. The only trouble is, once those materials become wet they won't work that well any more. Examples are sawdust, conifer needles, bark-mulch, sharp sand, stone meal, and woodash.

Slug ferment

This is probably one of the most disgusting slug control methods but one which is very effective. Collect a number of slugs in a bucket, pour boiling water over them and close the lid. It will start to smell horribly after about a week or two. You can then use it diluted with water (1:20) and sprinkle over all slug susceptible areas in your garden. Be careful, however, not to get the juice onto your vegetable plants. They wouldn't taste very nice after that. Good luck!

Catching slugs

Wooden boards:

You won't believe how many dedicated organic gardeners go out at night on a slug hunt. A much easier way to catch them is to place small wooden boards or slates around newly planted vegetables. The wooden boards provide shelter for slugs during the day so you can collect them first thing in the morning. It is absolutely necessary that you check the traps once a day otherwise you make the problem worse. I often found that after a few weeks some ground beetles have moved in under the boards. Once you have them, they will do the collection for you.

Bran:
Slugs adore bran and are attracted to it from all around your garden. If you want to lure them into one place so that you can collect them easily, place a couple of small piles of bran around the garden but make sure that you don't forget to collect them at night. There is a theory that slugs love bran so much that they stuff themselves with it and then it swells up inside them and they explode. I have never witnessed this spectacle so I'm not sure how true it is.

Slug poisons:
If the above methods don't work for you and you are desperate there is now an organically certified slug pellet on the market. It's called 'Ferramol'. Apparently it is completely harmless to any other creature.

Brassica problems

All members of the brassica family are susceptible to a wide variety of pests and diseases. Members of the brassica family include broccoli, Brussels sprouts, cauliflower, cabbage, calabrese, Chinese cabbage, kale, radish, swede, turnip and many oriental salads.

Brassica pests

Cabbage root fly

Description:
The cabbage root fly is a serious pest which affects most brassicas caused by the root fly's maggots which eat the roots of the brassicas. It is an ashy-grey fly about 0.5cm long resembling a small housefly. It produces two to three generations per year.

Symptoms:
Young plants look wilted and stop growing. The leaves develop a blue colour. When you pull up an infected plant, you will notice numerous white leg-less maggots about 2mm long feeding on the roots and afterwards tunnel through the stem of the plant.

Lifecycle:
The first generation of root fly emerges in April and May from over-wintered pupae. The females lay their eggs close to the stems of any brassica. These turn into maggots and start feeding on the roots and tunnel into the stems. The maggots mature within three weeks and turn into a small brown pupa a short distance away. After only a week a new generation emerges in search of more brassica plants. They continue breeding for the whole summer.

Prevention and control:
Once the root fly has laid their eggs at the base of the plants there is no organic control method available. To lessen the damage, place 15cm wide collars around newly planted brassicas. You can buy these in garden centres or use a piece of carpet underlay. The idea behind it is that the adult fly is prevented from laying its eggs at the stem. However, it doesn't always work. In wet years you may even create a slug breeding station under the collars!
The best prevention is to cover newly planted brassicas with a horticultural fleece or even better with bionet.

It also helps to start brassicas off in modules as they will develop a stronger root system before the attack. Earthing up the plants may also lessen the problem to a certain extent as they are able to produce more roots to compensate.

Caterpillars

Description:
True caterpillars are the larvae of moths and butterflies. They normally have three pairs of legs on the front segments of the body and a varying number of sucker feet on the rear segments.

These must be one of the best known and prolific of all garden pests. The caterpillars that affect brassicas include the Small and Large White Cabbage Butterfly and the Cabbage Moth.
There are generally two generations per year and they feed on all brassica plants including many wild ones.

Symptoms:
The Large White Butterfly usually lays all its eggs onto one plant. Clusters of yellow eggs can be found mostly on the underside of leaves. It has small, hairy, yellow and black caterpillars up to 5cm long. These are the most gregarious caterpillars decimating a plant in a few days, leaving just the midrib skeleton of the leaves.

The Small White Butterfly and the Cabbage Moth usually lay only one or two eggs on many plants. The caterpillars are usually light green and sometimes with a yellow stripe along its body. They mostly feed on the growing point of the plant. They are a lot more inconspicuous and thus much harder to spot and control. Cabbage Moth caterpillars are darker in colour and feed at night.

Control and prevention:
Regular hand removal of the eggs and caterpillars can be quite effective. It is, however, very time consuming and possibly not the nicest past-time!
The best prevention is to cover your brassicas throughout their growing season with a suitable netting. The netting can be laid directly over the crop or onto wire hoops like a cloche.
There is also a biological control available (Bacillus thuringiensis).

Flea beetles

Description:
Flea beetles are tiny black or blue-black beetles. They are difficult to see as they jump away like fleas when disturbed. They attack all brassicas and do most damage on turnip, radish, rocket, pak choi, mustard and cress.

Symptoms:
The adult beetles attack the leaves

of seedlings and small plants. Small holes (2-3mm across) are eaten out of the leaves. This will check the growth or even kill the plants. Many garden writers state that most damage is done in April/May and especially during dry weather.

I believe we have a different breed here in Ireland. In some years they are a problem until July and they certainly didn't seem to mind the wet.

Prevention and control:

There is very little you can do if they are already attacking your plants. As a prevention you can cover your plants with a suitable fine netting and properly pegged down at the sides. This has to be done straight after sowing or planting. When lifting the netting for weed control choose a windy day to take the smell of the brassicas away.

Bob Flowerdew has an interesting control method which I haven't tried yet. He coats one side of a piece of cardboard with treacle and waves it around above the affected plants. As the beetles jump when they are disturbed they stick onto the treacle and apparently his chickens are having a great time!

Mealy aphids

Description:

The adults of the mealy aphid are grey-green in colour and are covered with a powdering of white mealy wax. The aphids affect all brassicas, especially cabbages, Brussels sprouts, broccoli, cauliflowers and swedes.

Infestations can be severe from July until late October or even longer in mild weather. Aphids are also responsible for transmitting virus diseases from one plant to the other (e.g. turnip mosaic virus).

Symptoms:

Where the aphids are feeding, the leaves get discoloured and distorted. Severe infestations may seriously check growth and may even kill young and weak plants.

Prevention and control:

In order to come up with a preventative strategy we need to look at the lifecycle of the mealy aphid. The last generation of aphids lays eggs on brassica plants in autumn. The eggs overwinter and hatch in April. From May until July winged aphids are born and they establish new colonies on your newly planted brassicas. The best preventative method is not to let the eggs overwinter in your garden. I never allow any brassica in my garden after January and I make sure that any stalks or crop residue is collected and properly composted.

I appreciate that I will never have very early spring cabbages, but you'll be surprised how quickly an early spring sown crop can mature. Try to encourage ladybirds, hoverflies and lacewings into your garden as they all feed on aphids. As a direct control you should examine your plants regularly and squash any colony you find or alternatively use a certified organic spray such as Pyrethrum or insecticidal soap.

Cabbage whitefly

Description:
The cabbage whitefly is a small sap-feeding insect about 2mm long. The adults are pure white and usually found on the underside of the leaves. It only attacks members of the brassica family. It is very hardy, so it generally survives Irish winters quite easily.

Symptoms:
The underside of leaves is covered with the aphids, the honeydew they excude and often an infestation of sooty mould soon follows.

Prevention and control:
Use the same preventative strategy as for mealy aphids: break the cycle. It is also advisable to remove any yellowing leaves at the bottom. There may well be hundreds of aphid eggs on it. You can also wash off the whitefly, honeydew and sooty mould with a strong jet of water. Cabbage whitefly causes less damage than the other brassica pests.

Try to encourage beneficial insect such as ladybirds, hoverflies and lacewings into your garden.

Apart from the specific brassica pests (pests that only affect brassicas) a few more widespread pest will take a nibble or more of you brassicas. These include slugs, snails and pigeons.

Brassica diseases

Clubroot

Description:
Clubroot is probably the most difficult disease you may encounter in your garden. If you start a new garden the chances of having clubroot are slim and you can easily prevent it from entering. All brassicas may be affected by the disease. Once you have clubroot the cysts can survive for up to 9 years in the soil so normal rotations are of little use in eliminating clubroot. This means that you can't grow any brassicas for a very long time in this plot. It usually arrives into your garden from infected transplants or even by walking from an infected soil onto a clean patch. Clubroot is often commonplace in established allotment gardens whereas isolated vegetable gardens rarely have it.

Symptoms:
Typical symptoms of clubroot include poor growth, wilting leaves with reddish-purple colouration. When you pull out the roots you'll notice swollen, knobbly and deformed growth with a strongly unpleasant smell. In more advanced stages the roots will have rotted away into a slimy mess. Another name for clubroot is 'fingers and toes' which derives from its likeness to advanced arthritis.

Prevention and control:
Once you have clubroot in your garden you will have to live with it. There are now a few clubroot resistant varieties available and more of them will be developed.
Whilst you can't get rid of the disease you can minimise the problem by:
- not composting your brassica roots (dispose of them or burn them)
- not sowing a brassica green manure (mustard, rape)
- starting the plants in modules and even potting them on into small pots
- liming the soil the previous autumn (clubroot thrives in acidic conditions)
- growing in raised beds (clubroot prefers wet soils)

A cabbage collar for preventing cabbage root fly

Tools

Buying tools

In my gardening life there is nothing more irritating than a bad tool. They annoy you every single day until they hopefully break. Unfortunately good tools are a rarity nowadays, but there are still some excellent suppliers and garden centres that stock good ones. Unfortunately, my best friends – good hoes – can only be got from good suppliers.

Other good places to look for tools are car boot sales or markets. The old tools were made to last and they can easily be done up again.

Good tools are an excellent investment. It is far better to start off with the few essential ones and to buy the best rather than to buy a whole set of an inferior quality.

For starting a small vegetable plot there is no need to buy a large range of fancy gardening tools. The following tools are sufficient.

Spade

The first tool you need to buy is a good spade. Look out for one with a stainless steel blade. It will lighten the work, is easy to clean and will last forever. I always prefer the smaller or medium sized spades as they are a lot easier to handle compared to the big builder's ones. If you hit the blade with your knuckles and it gives a ringing sound, you know it's good quality.

Also make sure that the handle has a comfortable grip and is of the right length for your height.

Digging is hard enough so you may as well get a comfortable tool.

I bought a good stainless steel spade about ten years ago for about €50 and I'm sure it will last another ten years. You can get cheap ones for about €20 but I doubt if they will last.

Uses: digging, planting, skimming off weeds, composting.

Fork

The most useful fork is the one with four flat prongs which can be used like a spade especially on stony ground and heavy clay soils. In Ireland the one with four curved prongs is also very popular, but be careful on heavy stony ground as the prongs tend to bend. I use the curved type for composting, spreading manure and even some light digging.

Uses: Digging, handling compost, loosening and aerating soil, digging out root crops, breaking down rough dug soil.

Rake

The rake is another essential equipment. It is vital for preparing seed beds. Make sure the handle is smooth and long enough (1.5m) and that the teeth are very solidly fitted to the head.

Uses: Preparing seed beds, levelling soil, breaking down lumps, raking up leaves, stones etc.

Hoe

Hoeing is probably one of the most important organic gardening activities. If you get this right you can save yourselves hours of unnecessary work. Hoe as much as you can when the weather is dry, but never too deeply. I have a few favourite hoes, but one will be enough for a beginner.

Oscillating hoe (125mm) from Fruit Hill Farm

Round hoe (130mm) from Fruit Hill Farm

Sorry for advertising here but these hoes are only available from this company and their agents across the country. I think every garden centre should stock them, so please ask, so they will in the future.

Wheelbarrow

A wheelbarrow is an essential for all but the very smallest gardens. It is useful for all sorts of materials around the garden.

Small hand tools

Garden centres sell a massive range of small hand tools for many different purposes. The only ones you most definitely need are a hand trowel and hand fork. Stainless steel tools are a lot better, but also a lot pricier.

The trowel is used for planting out small plants and for digging up deep-rooted weeds such as dandelions. The hand fork is used for digging out weeds and scuffling the soil surface around plants to break up surface compaction.

Garden line

Get two small but strong stakes (about 50cm long) and connect with a long piece of string.

Without a garden line it is very difficult to make up straight beds or sow your vegetables in straight rows.

Measuring rod

Get a piece of timber 2m long (5cm x 2.5cm) and mark it into useful measurements (20, 30, 40cm)

Use: for planting out vegetables at accurate spacing.

Watering can or hosepipe

Watering is rarely necessary outdoors in the West of Ireland. The only time you may need to water is after transplanting your seedlings outdoors. You will need a small watering can with a fine rose for watering your trays of seedlings and a normal one for your outdoor vegetables.

Tool care and maintenance

It is very good practice to wash your tools after use and store them in a dry shed. The handles should be oiled with boiled linseed oil once or twice a year and I usually soak rusty tools in a mixture of waste oil and diesel for a while over winter. Alternatively you can brush the mix onto the blades.

Checklist of other items you'll need:

Seeds (ideally organic seeds)

Ideally you order or buy your seeds well before the growing season starts as soon as you have finished your plan.

Onion sets, garlic bulbs and seed potatoes

There is often a shortage of organic onion sets, garlic and seed potatoes. Thus it is important to buy or order them early. I would always opt for organic plant material if the quality is good. If the quality is poorer I would rather buy it conventionally from a garden centre. Remember if you plant poor quality you will most likely harvest poor quality.

Seed compost (ideally organic and peat-free)

For sowing your seeds you should purchase a seed compost.

Please be aware: a lot of suppliers have jumped the bandwagon about 'organics'. There are numerous compost and fertiliser products around at every garden centre throughout the country which are sold as organic. The majority of them are not organic!!! If you are in doubt ask the garden centre with which certifying body the product is registered. If it is not certified with any certification body it is not organic.

I feel this is a very aggravating promotional technique of some large companies who want to mislead gardeners into thinking they are doing something good and charge them extra for it. They are not doing anything illegal, though, as the term 'organic' is only legally protected in relation to food.

Some growers make their own seed compost, but I would not recommend this for beginners. It's not easy to get the mixture right and a year's growing depends on it. There are a few good certified organic seed composts available including a peat free medium. If you can't get organic seed compost in your locality don't opt for the very coarse multi-purpose compost but better buy a specialist fine-grained seed compost.

Potting compost (ideally peat free compost)

Potting compost is useful for potting on small plants, especially if the weather conditions don't allow you to plant them out in time. I would opt for a peat free compost. The difference between a peat free and peat based medium is that you may have to water the peat free compost more regularly as it can't hold as much water.

An area for propagation

It is essential that you allocate an area for plant raising. This may be in a greenhouse with or without a propagator, in a polytunnel or even your south-facing windowsills. If you haven't much propagation space you may be able to sow most crops directly outside.

A hardening off area

Imagine coming out of your warm house into the cold and wind with no extra clothes on. That is exactly how your little plants feel. You have to acclimatise them.

Pots and trays

Before you start you should have a sufficient number of pots and modular trays. Especially in the case of modular trays you pay for what you get. You can buy very cheap ones which you throw away after use or buy more expensive ones which will last you for years.

A trailer load of old/ancient manure or compost

It is very important to think of this even before you start digging. This is for your soil fertility, the nutrients, the worms etc. You can't start a garden organically without that trailer load full of goodness!

Bamboo canes or hazel rods

If you want to grow peas and runner beans you need to provide them with a strong climbing support. Other plants that may need some sort of support include broad beans, Brussels sprouts.

Optional items

Crop cover (fleece or bionet)
Windbreak netting
Hedging plants (for windbreaks)

Month by Month Guide

January

January is the best month to sit inside and plan your vegetable garden. It's always a good idea to look back at the last year and evaluate what did well and what needs improvement. If you haven't got a diary yet you should really get one to record your cropping plan, your vegetable varieties, sowing and harvesting dates.

It is also a good time to order your seeds, seed potatoes and onion sets. I get a lot pleasure browsing through various mail order seed catalogues. I always prefer to have the seeds ordered well before I need them. You will find a list of seed suppliers at the end of the book. Nearly all seed catalogues are free of charge and you can shop around for the best varieties and price.

It is wise to plan your vegetable garden well in advance. The more thorough your plan the easier you will find the work throughout the year. The ideal would be to have a sowing plan so you know exactly what to sow, how much of it and where you will plant it.

Check all your stored vegetables and discard any bad ones to prevent them from spreading throughout.

Clean your tools. After cleaning use boiled linseed oil for wooden handles and a mixture of oil and diesel to get rid rust on metal blades.

Harvesting
Harvesting outdoors: Jerusalem artichokes, parsnips, Brussels sprouts, winter cabbage, leeks and kale.
Use stored vegetables: potatoes, beetroot, Dutch cabbage, carrots, marrows, onions, garlic shallots and swedes.

February

Despite the fact that the days are noticeably longer, February is

261

nevertheless a very cold month. If it is reasonably dry, however, you can start getting a few beds ready especially the ones needed for the early sown or planted crops (broad beans, Jerusalem artichokes, early potatoes, onions, shallots and garlic).

If you haven't washed out your seed trays or pots now is a good time to do it.

Chit your early potatoes now.

Sowing

Autumn leeks can be sown in the middle of the month if you have a propagator or suitable indoor space. Leeks take about 8 to 10 weeks from sowing to planting out. An early sowing is only suitable if you have a greenhouse or a tunnel to keep them in until you plant them.

Towards the end of the month you can sow broad beans and plant Jerusalem artichokes and garlic weather permitting. Never sow or plant if the ground is frosty or too wet. You do more damage than good.

Harvesting

Harvesting outdoors: Jerusalem artichokes, parsnips, Brussels sprouts, winter cabbage, leeks and kale.

Use stored vegetables: potatoes, beetroot, Dutch cabbage, carrots, marrows, onions, garlic, shallots, swedes.

March

Don't be misled by the nice spells of weather we often get in March. Apart from the few vegetables listed below there is nothing you can sow or plant outdoors.

Continue preparing beds if there is a dry spell. Rake over the beds you have prepared last month to get rid of weed seedlings. You should also check your stored vegetables for any signs of rot.

Sowing

Around the middle of the month you can plant your early potatoes, onion and shallot sets. To protect your onion and shallot sets from birds you can cover them with bird netting over wire hoops or alternatively cover with a cloche covered in bionet.

Sow indoors in a tunnel or windowsill: leeks, early cabbage, scallions, celery and celeriac.

If you haven't sown broad beans yet there is till time.

Jerusalem artichokes and garlic can also still be planted.

Harvesting

Harvest outdoors: Jerusalem artichokes, parsnips, leeks, kale and possibly perpetual spinach which is re-sprouting again. All these crops are slowly coming to an end now so you should use them up quickly if you have many of them left. You will soon get your first picking of purple sprouting broccoli this month.

Use stored vegetables: potatoes, beetroot, Dutch cabbage, carrots, onions, shallots and swedes.

April

April is a busy month. You should try to have all the beds prepared even if you don't plant anything yet. This allows you to control the weeds before the crops go in (see weed control). Give the prepared beds a sprinkle of seaweed dust and rake it in.

Keep an eye out for slugs. They are starting to get busy.

Sowing

The soil is starting to warm up but it is still far too early to sow directly outside for most crops . However you will be very busy sowing seeds indoors and cluttering up your windowsills or filling your greenhouse with seed trays.

Outdoor sowing and planting:

The only vegetables I sow directly outdoors in April are early peas, radish and turnips. If you haven't got enough propagation space you can sow spinach and chard directly outside instead of raising it in modules.

Mid April is a good time to plant your maincrop potatoes. If you haven't planted your onion and shallot sets yet you can still plant them now.

In the warmer parts of the country you can sow your early carrots, early beetroot and parsnips but I always have a lot more success with these if I delay the sowing until May.

April is also a good month to start your asparagus bed.

Indoor sowing:

Seeds which can be sown indoors include winter leeks, cabbage, cauliflower, Brussels sprouts, calabrese, kohlrabi, rocket, swede, turnip, lettuce, perpetual spinach, chard, annual spinach and scallions

Indoor sowing with heat:

Courgette, pumpkin, squash, French bean, runner bean and sweetcorn can be sown in small pots at the end of the month and leave them on a warm south-facing windowsill.

Planting

When the soil conditions are favourable you can plant out scallions and early cabbages.

Harvesting

April is the beginning of the 'Hungry Gap' period where the winter vegetables are going and no new crop is ready. You may still have a few root vegetables in store (potato, carrot, beetroot and parsnip) and outside you may pick purple sprouting broccoli and some perpetual spinach and chard.

May

May is definitely the busiest month in your vegetable garden and hopefully you have managed to do all the other jobs such as bed preparation in the previous months. The soil has warmed up sufficiently to sow and plant nearly all vegetables. So make sure you take time off in May so that you can spend days in the garden!

Finish preparing the beds and keep the hoe and rake moving over them. Watch out for late frosts and have some horticultural fleece handy to cover your potatoes if needed. You should thin out your emerging seedlings to the correct spacing.

Sowing

Outdoor sowing:
In the first half of May you can sow early beetroot, early carrots, parsnips, perpetual spinach, annual spinach, chard, radish, turnip, peas and runner beans directly into the ground.

Towards the end of the month you can sow maincrop carrots and beetroot and any crops you didn't manage to sow at the beginning of the month.

Indoor sowing:
In May you can still sow the following vegetables into modular trays: winter cabbages, Brussels sprouts, calabrese, kale, kohlrabi, swede, turnip, lettuce, scallions, spinach and chard.

If you haven't sown courgettes, pumpkins, squash, runner beans and sweetcorn yet you can still do so at the first half of the month.

Towards the end of the month you can sow Florence fennel and Chinese cabbage.

Planting
You can plant out the crops you sowed in the previous month: the first batch of leeks, cabbage, cauliflower, Brussels sprouts, calabrese, kohlrabi, rocket, swede, turnip, lettuce, perpetual spinach, chard, annual spinach and scallions.

Harvesting
Towards the end of the month you may be able to harvest some oriental salads, radish, turnips and annual spinach.

Pest watch
Don't forget to keep a check on your plants especially the seedlings outside. This is the time when they are most vulnerable to a slug attack. You also need to be wary

of leatherjackets, the larva of the daddy-longlegs. They can be a terror during this month especially on newly planted lettuce. If a small lettuce suddenly dies, it was probably eaten by a leather-jacket. They actually just bite through the stem of the young plants. If you don't find the culprit in the soil it will move on to the next plant.

If you had carrot root fly in previous years it is nearly essential that you cover the early sown carrots with a bionet.

June

Apart from a few more sowings and plantings there is relatively little to do in the garden apart from maintaining your crops.

Keep hoeing and weeding. Your plants are still at a vulnerable stage where they can very easily get swamped by weeds.

Thin all your direct sown vegetables when they are still quite small to the required spacing. If you neglect thinning you will only be able to harvest tiny and often mis-shaped vegetables. You should not replant thinnings especially from root crops.

During dry spells you may have to water your outdoor seedlings.

Sowing

Outdoor sowing:

You can still sow carrots, beetroot and peas if you missed the sowing in May. And you can continue with successional sowings of radish, turnip and annual spinach.

Indoor sowing:

You can still sow kohlrabi, Chinese cabbage, Florence fennel, oriental salads, lettuce, and scallions into modular trays.

June is a good time to sow your purple sprouting broccoli.

Planting

You can plant out your late leeks, winter cabbages, Brussels sprouts, calabrese, kale, kohlrabi, swede, turnip, lettuce, scallions, celery, celeriac, spinach and chard.

Early June is also the best time to plant out your courgettes, squash, pumpkin, sweetcorn, French beans and runner beans after they have been hardened off. Only plant them out if it is warm. They would benefit from a cloche for the first few weeks.

Harvesting

Finally you can get a reasonable harvest from your garden. You may have some lettuce, scallions, radish, turnip, early cabbage, early potatoes (towards the end of the month), early peas, broad beans, spinach and chard.

Pest watch

Watch out for the cabbage white butterflies. When you see them flying around you should check the undersides of any brassica leaves and look out for the small yellow eggs which turn into caterpillars and ruin your plants. The earlier you spot and remove them the better.

July

In theory, July should be a dry month but this is not always the case in Ireland. If we do get a dry summer you might have to water. If you water your plants give them a thorough soaking. Watering little and often is a disaster as it brings the plant roots up instead of encouraging them to go down.

Keep your beds well hoed and weeded. Thin out all direct sown vegetables to the recommended spacing even if you have to pull out ten seedlings while leaving just one.

As soon as your early potatoes are harvested you may consider sowing a green manure crop into its place to stop nutrients from leaching out. I think phacelia is the most suited crop for this time.

Harvesting

In July there is plenty to harvest from your garden and hopefully you are at home to enjoy the feast. You will have broad beans, dwarf French beans, runner beans, cabbage, courgettes, kohlrabi, lettuce, scallions, peas, early potatoes, radish, spinach, chard and turnips.

Sowing

You can still sow lettuce, scallions, kohlrabi, turnip, radish, Chinese cabbage and Florence fennel.

Planting

You can plant out the crops that were sown in the previous month. Also plant out kale, calabrese, perpetual spinach, chard, Chinese cabbage, Florence fennel, kohlrabi, lettuce and scallions.

Pest watch

Aphids tend to be a problem in mid summer especially in more sheltered gardens. Watch out for ladybirds or hoverflies as they may already control them. If aphids are a big problem they can be sprayed with pyrethrum or soft soap, but both sprays will also harm ladybirds. Aphids can also be washed off plants with a strong jet of water. Keep checking your brassicas for butterfly eggs.

August

August is a relatively quiet month in your vegetable garden. You can sit back, relax and enjoy the fruits of your labour. As soon as you have harvested and cleared a bed you should consider re-planting it or sowing a green manure crop. Keep on top of the weeds.

Sowing

There are only a few vegetables you can still sow in August: lettuce (especially loose-leaf types or Little Gem), scallions, radishes, baby turnips, annual spinach. August is the best month to sow all your winter salads. They prefer to grow in the latter half of the year. The best ones are rocket, mizuna, mustard 'Red Frills' and 'Green Wave', pak choy, claytonia, tatsoi and corn salad.

If you wish to grow over-wintering spring cabbage now is the time to sow it.

Planting

You can plant out lettuce, scallions, kohlrabi, turnip, Chinese cabbage Florence fennel.

Harvesting

Your garden should yield plentiful in August.

You should still have broad beans, dwarf French beans, runner beans, cabbage, calabrese, cauliflower, courgettes, marrow, kohlrabi, lettuce, scallions, peas, early potatoes, radish, spinach, chard and turnips.

You can start pulling some of your early carrots and beetroot. At this stage never harvest more than you need for a few days.

Garlic is usually ready for harvesting towards the end of the month. Wait until the leaves have turned yellow but are still standing. Fork the bulbs out very gently and dry them thoroughly ideally in the sun.

Pest watch

Keep checking for pest damage especially on your brassicas.

September

In September we often have the best weather and the harvest is even more abundant.

Broad beans and early peas are likely to be finished by now. You can either pull out the crop or cut them off at ground level to keep the nitrogen they have fixed in the ground. I don't think it makes a big difference as you just move the nitrogen into the compost and at a later stage spread it out in the garden again.

You can now sow an over-wintering green manure crop such

as grazing rye/vetch mix or field beans (only towards the end of the month)

Sowing
The only crops you can still sow in September are the hardy winter salads. There is a large range of them available. My favourites ones are rocket, mizuna, mustard 'Red Frills' and 'Green Wave', pak choy, claytonia, tatsoi and corn salad.

Planting
You can plant out lettuce, scallions, turnips, annual spinach, spring cabbage and all your winter salads. Over-wintering onion sets can be planted now.

Harvesting
You can still harvest early carrots beetroot, dwarf French beans, runner beans, cabbage, calabrese, cauliflower, courgettes, marrow, kohlrabi, lettuce, scallions, peas, early potatoes, radish, spinach, chard and turnips.

New vegetables to harvest this month are kale and leeks.

Sometime in September you harvest all your onions. Wait until most of the leaves have turned yellow and have fallen over. Then pull them out of the ground and let them dry in the sun.

If you have attempted to grow sweetcorn you should check the cobs now. Just lift the husk a little bit and see if the kernels have turned yellow.

October

October is the month to fill your larder. Many crops are harvested and stored safely for the long winter months. It's also the month to put your beds to bed for the winter.

As the ground becomes vacant after harvesting crops you can put the beds to bed for the winter. A thick cover of fresh seaweed is ideal. If you can't get any seaweed you should either cover the beds with strong black plastic or grow an overwintering green manure crop. The most efficient method is to prepare the beds and work in some compost and then cover the beds securely with black plastic. You will have very little work to do in the following spring. It is advisable to get as much of this work done before the weather turns unpleasant.

Stake tall brassicas such as kale, Brussels sprouts and purple sprouting broccoli to prevent them from rocking and collapsing in the wind.

Sowing
You may think it's far too late to sow any vegetables so late in the year. In actual fact it is the ideal time to sow your overwintering broad beans and to plant you over-wintering garlic. Just make sure

that you use suitable varieties. October is still a good month to sow green manures. You can sow grazing rye, vetch and field beans.

Harvesting

Harvest all your maincrop potatoes. Dig them out carefully, let them dry for an hour and then store them. Never wash them before storage.

You can also dig out your carrots and beetroot and store them in boxes of sand in a frost free shed. The firm Dutch cabbages should also be harvested and stored in a cool shed but not in sand.

Celeriac, parsnips, leeks, savoy cabbage, kohlrabi, perpetual spinach and swede can be harvested as required. They can be left outdoors as they are very hardy. However, if your ground becomes very waterlogged in winter you better dig out your parsnips, swedes and celeriac at the end of the month and store them in boxes of sand. The first brussels sprouts may be ready by now.

The runner beans are probably finished by now. After your last picking you can clear the plants. It helps if you chop or cut the stems before putting them on the compost heap. If you leave the roots in the ground the nitrogen rich nodules will stay in the ground.

November

November is often a miserable month for gardening. Luckily there isn't much to do outside apart from harvesting for the kitchen and continuing to cover the beds.

Your compost heap will benefit from turning. It is important that the heap is covered especially over the winter months to prevent leaching of nutrients which is caused by excessive rain.

Collect as many autumn leaves as possible and store them in a leafmould cage near your compost heap. They can be used in the following year in your compost heap mixed with lawn mowings. Continue making up beds and covering them with black plastic.

Sowing

In case you have missed the October sowing of broad beans and garlic you can still sow or plant them at the beginning of the month.

It is possibly too late to sow green manures now and get enough growth before the winter. The only exceptions are field beans and grazing rye which should do okay from an early November sowing.

Harvesting

In your store you will have Dutch cabbage, carrots, beetroot and potatoes. Outdoors you can harvest leeks, Jerusalem artichokes, winter cabbages, Brussels sprouts, kale, parsnip, celeriac, swede and possibly some perpetual spinach.

December

General jobs in the garden

Many seed companies send out their new mail order seed catalogues in December. Nearly all of them are free of charge. You can compare varieties, prices and seasonality. It is good to have all seeds bought before the beginning of the growing season.

Never leave your soil bare over the winter. The excessive rainfall in winter will cause excessive leaching of nutrients and often creates a swamp. Prepare the beds, add compost and cover any remaining beds with black plastic.

Sowing

There is nothing you can sow or plant in December.

Harvesting

In December you will have carrots, beetroot, potatoes and Dutch cabbage from your storage shed. Outdoors you can harvest leeks, Jerusalem artichokes, winter cabbages, Brussels sprouts, kale, parsnip, celeriac and swede. It might be more convenient for you to harvest the remaining parsnips, celeriac and swede and store them in boxes of sand in a frost free shed.

It is worth checking the vegetables you have in store and remove any rotten ones to stop the disease from spreading.

Glossary

Acid – A soil with a pH of below 7.

Aerobic – A process which takes place in the presence of air.

Alkaline – A soil with a pH of over 7.

Anaerobic – A process which takes place without air.

Annual – A plant that completes its lifecycle from seed to seed in one year.

Bare-rooted – A plant lifted from the soil as opposed to a potted plant.

Beneficial insect – An insect that preys on pests or diseases or assists in plant pollination.

Biennial – A plant that completes its lifecycle from seed to seed in a two-year period.

Biological control – A method of controlling pests by the introduction of a predator.

Blanching – In gardening terms it means to exclude light from the plants, either the whole plant or the leaves and stems.

Bolting – The premature production of flowers and seeds.

Broadcast – A sowing technique whereby seeds are scattered and raked into the soil.

Capping – A crust that forms on the surface of certain soils, often as a cause of compaction or heavy rainfall followed by quick drying.

Catch crop – A catch crop refers to a quick growing crop that is sown amongst slow growing vegetables to make the maximum use of space.

Clamp – A structure made of earth for storing root vegetables outdoors.

Cloche – A movable structure traditionally made of a metal frame and glass panes. Cloches nowadays come in many designs, mostly in plastic or netting.

Cold frame – A rectangular box with a glass or plastic lid used for propagation and hardening off.

Cotyledon – The first leaves produced by a seedling.

Deficiency – An adverse condition in plants that is caused by a shortage of one or more plant nutrients.

Direct sowing – Where seeds are sown directly into the open ground rather than raised indoors in trays or pots.

Disorder – An adverse condition in plants that is commonly caused by environmental factors.

Double digging – Method of digging to a depth of two spades without bringing the subsoil up to the surface.

Drill – A shallow trench or furrow in which seeds are sown.

Earthing up – To draw soil around the base of a plant for support, for increasing the growing space or for blanching purposes.

Erosion – The process of soil being washed away or blown off the surface of the ground.

F1 Hybrid – F1 refers to "first filial" or first generation offspring from two pure bred parents.

Foliar feeding – An application of liquid fertiliser to the plant foliage.

Friable – Describes a soil that is crumbly and capable of forming a tilth.

Genetic engineering – The mechanical transfer of DNA.

Germination – The development of a seed into a seedling.

Green manure – A crop which is grown with the purpose of improving the soil in terms of nutrient content and/or structure. A green manure crop is always incorporated where it has grown.

Half hardy – Plants that can tolerate low temperatures but not frost.

Hardy – Plants which can withstand frost without protection.

Hardening off – To acclimatise plants gradually to cooler conditions. This is especially important for plants that were raised in warm conditions.

Haulm – The leaves (foliage) of plants such as potatoes.

Herbicide – A weedkiller.

Hybrid – The offspring of a cross between two or more varieties, usually of the same species.

Humus – The fragrant, spongy, nutrient-rich material resulting from de-composition of organic matter.

Intercropping – Mixing different vegetables in the same bed.

Leaching – The downward washing and loss of soluble nutrients from the topsoil.

Legume – Vegetables of the Leguminosae family, e.g. peas and beans. They have the ability to take up nitrogen from the air.

Natural enemy – One creature or organism that preys upon another.

Nematode – A microscopic eelworm.

Nitrogen – One of the main plant nutrients. Used for the growth of leaves and shoots.

Nutrient – A plant food.

Modules – Moulded trays which are divided up into individual cells. The cells are filled with seed compost and seeds can be sown individually and planted out with minimum soil disturbance.

Mulch – A layer of an organic or inorganic material laid over the ground for the purpose of controlling weeds and protecting the soil surface.

Open pollinated – A non-hybrid variety, one that can reproduce itself.

Organic matter – A material which derives and consists of living organisms either dead or alive.

pH – The units by which the degree of acidity or alkalinity is measured.

Perennial – A non-woody plant that has a lifecycle of over three years. A herbaceous perennial dies back and becomes dormant in winter and grows again in the following spring.

Pesticide – A product that will kill pests, diseases or weeds.

Pheromone – A chemical substance which is secreted by animals and affects the behaviour of other animals.

Phosphate – A phosphorus compound (P_2O_5).

Phosphorus – Major plant nutrient, especially important for root growth.

Pinch out – Removal of growing tip of a plant to encourage branching.

Pollination – Transfer of pollen to the stigma of a flower to fertilise it.

Potash – A potassium compound (K_2O).

Potassium – Major plant nutrient especially important for flower and fruit development.

Predator – An animal that eats other animals.

Prick out – To transfer seedlings from a seed tray into a pot or seedbed.

Resistance – This implies that a variety of vegetable will resist disease when exposed to a disease-causing pathogen.

Rotation – A system where crops are grouped into plant families and grown in different plots on a 3-4 year cycle. This limits the build up of soil-borne pests and diseases and makes the best use of soil nutrients.

Rotavator – A machine with rotating blades which break up the soil.

Soil conditioner – Material that improves the structure of a soil.

Spore – The reproductive body of a fungus.

Subsoil – The soil layer below the topsoil also called B-horizon.

Tap root – A strong growing, vertical root as in carrot or dandelion.

Tilth – The fine, crumbly structure on the soil surface.

Tolerance – Tolerance implies that a variety of vegetable will perform relatively well when exposed to environmental stresses.

Top-dressing – Application of organic matter onto the soil surface.

Trace elements – A plant nutrient which plants require in very small quantities.

Variety – A genetically similar population of plants, distinct in one or more traits from other populations.

Water table – The level of the soil below which the soil is saturated by ground water.

Useful Contacts

Organic training institutions

The Organic Centre
Rossinver
Co. Leitrim
Tel: 071 9854338
www.theorganiccentre.ie

An Tionad Glas Organic College
Dromcollogher
Co. Limerick
www.organiccollege.com

Western Organic Network
Drumshanbo
Co. Leitrim
www.westernorganicnetwork.com

National Organic Training Services (NOTS)
Drumshanbo
Co. Leitrim
www.nots.ie

Croghan Organic Garden
Co. Roscommon
Tel: 071 9668963
www.croghanorganicgardens.ie

Huntingbrook Gardens
Blessington
Co. Wicklow
www.huntingbrook.com

Nano Nagle Birthplace
www.nanonaglebirthplace.ie

Irish organic certification bodies

I.O.F.G.A (Irish Organic Farmers and Growers Association)
www.iofga.ie

Organic Trust
www.organic-trust.ie

Tools and equipment

Fruit Hill Farm
Co. Cork
www.fruithillfarm.com

Envirogrind Compost
Co. Donegal
www.envirogrindltd.com

Quickcrop
Co. Sligo
For tools, veg plants and instant vegetable gardens
www.quickcrop.ie

Ardcarne Garden Centre
Co. Roscommon
www.plantsplus.ie/ardcarne-boyle

Springmount Garden Centre
Co. Wexford
www.springmount.ie

Gardening Maintenance & Landscaping

Feeneys Garden Centre
Co. Sligo
086 8553250

Holland Gardens
087 7792792/071 91 63786

Ardcarne Garden Centre
Boyle
Co Roscommon

Jeffery & Son
087 6664180

Poultry

Julian Pawlowski
Tawley
Co. Leitrim
087 6240811

Useful websites

GIY—Grow it Yourself
A wonderful charity which aims to inspire people
to grow their own food and give them the skills needed
to do so successfully
www.giyireland.com

Cultivate
Dublin
www.cultivate.ie

Irish Allotment Association
www.allotments.ie

Irish Garden Website
www.gardening.ie

Seed Suppliers

The Organic Centre
Co. Leitrim
www.theorganiccentre.ie

Irish Seed Saver Association
Co. Clare
www.irishseedsavers.ie

Thomas Etty Esq.
www.thomasetty.co.uk
They have an excellent variety of organic and heritage seeds

Eco Seeds (wildflowers)
www.ecoseeds.co.uk

Tamar Organics
www.tamarorganics.co.uk

Chiltern Seeds
www.chilternseed.co.uk

Edwin Tucker & Sons
www.tuckers-seeds.co.uk

Terre de Semences
www.terredesemence.com

Wallis Seeds
www.wallis-seeds.co.uk

Thompson & Morgan Seeds
www.thompson-morgan.com

CN Seeds
www.cnseeds.demon.co.uk

Suffolk Herbs
www.suffolkherbs.com
Brown Envelope Seeds
West Cork
www.brownenvelopeseeds.com

The Organic Gardening Catalogue
www.OrganicCatalog.com

UK Organic Associations

HDRA (Henry Doubleday Research Association)
They have a very informative website
www.hdra.org.uk

Soil Association
Largest organic association in the UK, excellent website
www.soilassociation.org

Biodynamic Association
www.anth.org.uk/biodynamic

Acknowledgements

Many thanks to my family for their inspiration, patience and support.

I'm indebted to Ray Warner from Thomas Etty Esquire Heritage Seed Company for allowing me use the beautiful Victorian illustrations of vegetables.

Many thanks also to Margaret for all her wisdom and interesting anecdotes.

There is no way to express my gratitude to my wife Joanna who really made it all possible and contributed tirelessly.

Index